Getting the Buggers in Tune

Also available from Continuum:

Getting the Buggers in Tune

IAN McCORMACK AND
JEANETTE HEALEY

continuum

Continuum International Publishing Group

The Tower Building	80 Maiden Lane
11 York Road	Suite 704
London SE1 7NX	New York
	NY 10038

www.continuumbooks.com

British Library Cataloguing-in-Publication Data
A catalogue record for this book is available from the British Library.

ISBN: 978-0-826-49439-9 (paperback)

Library of Congress Cataloging-in-Publication Data
A catalog record for this book is available from the Library of Congress.

Typeset by BookEns Ltd, Royston, Herts.
Printed and bound in Great Britain by MPG Books Ltd.

Contents

Chapter 4: The Importance of Music and the Creative Process   54

Chapter 5: Music Across the Curriculum   63

Acknowledgements

We would like to thank our families and friends for their support during this project: Roy for his computer; Jean for the childcare; Marcia for the coffee; David for the use of his Mac; and Kate for the endless phone calls and computer care.

In addition, we would like to thank Alexandra at Continuum for her understanding and advice, Ronald Frost (organist and choirmaster at St Ann's Church, Manchester and former lecturer at RNCM), Keith Havercroft (Schools Improvement Officer, Music and E learning, Shropshire County Council), David Healey (music producer), Gwyn Lloyd-Jones (headteacher), Jean Merrifield (music coordinator), Helen Monks (SLS vocal coach), Zoë Morris (Director of Arts College, Chorlton High School, Manchester), Naomi Elliott-Newman (north-west pathfinder coordinator – Hallé Orchestra), Lis Murphy (Drake Music Project), Rachael Parsons (primary teacher), Adrian Price (Soundbeam®), Gerrie Shadwell (Head of Arts College, Bridgewater High School, Warrington), Bernie Snagg (Arts College Technical Support, Bridgewater High School), Lorraine Suddaby (primary teacher).

Finally, thanks to all the children for their quotes and anyone else we may have forgotten.

INTRODUCTION

In a world constantly made smaller by technology we repeatedly hear about the problems caused by an inability to communicate. In 1887 Esperanto, a mixture of the chief European languages, was invented by a Polish physician as an international medium of communication. Despite his lofty ambitions Esperanto failed to live up to the hope implied by its name and today, over one hundred years later, the search continues.

There are of course those who will tell you that such a language already exists, that it can be understood the world over, that it avoids all cultural bias and confusion and is entirely unambiguous. The language they refer to is the language of number, or more accurately, mathematics. Often, however, those who so keenly espouse this language are already mathematicians themselves and find it hard to see that their definition of language is somewhat esoteric. There is no doubt that the concept of number is international but to say that its appreciation is universal falls somewhat short of the truth and completely ignores the fact that the joy and emotions it inspires are restricted in their appeal, often to those who have a special and particular passion for the world of numbers.

If we are to find an international language we must look for something that more effectively and more universally communicates the ideas, concepts and most of all the emotions that are so important to life and social interaction. The more we look the more apparent it becomes that the task, if not impossible, is Herculean in its scale and whatever answer we come up with seems bound to have drawbacks. Music as an answer is no exception to this rule but the more we think about it the more apparent it becomes that while it may not be the perfect answer, music may well win the day by being the candidate best suited to the purpose.

All of us, at some time or another, have had a favourite tune, or one that we have shared with that special someone. All of us have been haunted by a melody that spins, sometimes to the point of torment, around our head for hours or even days. Music can make the abstract concrete, or vice versa. It lifts the spirit or brings a tear to the eye. It can paint pictures, it can celebrate and it can mourn. It can say more eloquently, in a simple phrase, more than many of us can say in a hundred words. Music, if not a universal language, can transcend language. Through its infinite styles and genres it can help us share a moment when language deserts us.

The gift given by music to performer or audience is infinite because, although it speaks to many, it invites response from the individual. The deaf can respond to its rhythms and vibrations; it can unlock the world for the sightless, and give stimulation to those otherwise disabled. Music can lead us into other worlds; it can spark imagination and prompt enquiry. It can raise self-esteem, soothe turmoil, promote teamwork, stimulate intellect and so much more. Music is not just a tool for education – it is vital to it. Through this book we hope to show the many ways it can help our children and enrich their lives and their learning.

The title of this chapter is somewhat misleading in that it invites the inference that there is one single, universal National Curriculum for the whole of the English-speaking world. Clearly this is not and could not be the case. However, what is true is that music and its importance to the education of young people is acknowledged throughout the world.

In Australia and New Zealand, music provision in schools has recently been the subject of extensive research and review, and in both countries funding has been increased and the position of music confirmed as a vital part of the school curriculum.

In Australia research programmes have identified strong links between the study of music and improved performance in mathematics. The *Nation Review of School Music* in 2005 emphasized benefits such as enhanced language development, holistic development of aesthetic and kinaesthetic skills, improved social skills, improved appreciation of other cultures, raised self-esteem and enhanced communication skills.

In New Zealand a similar review, *Arts Education in New Zealand* (2000), was equally clear in its support of music in the National Curriculum and concluded that:

> Music education provides students with many opportunities for self-expression and assists them to develop to their full potential.

In the UK, while music is a statutory part of education in all of the constituent countries, separate legislation exists for each of England, Wales, Northern Ireland and Scotland.

The curriculum provision that appears to be most distinctly different is that of Scotland in that it combines the teaching of music to pupils aged 5–14 with PE, drama and art and design in an area of the curriculum called 'expressive arts'. Furthermore the general description of the curriculum and its content for pupils aged 5–14 is split into six sections, referred to as 'levels' and labelled from A to F.

By contrast the curriculum summaries for England, Wales and Northern Ireland restrict themselves to three broad areas that relate to the age groups for Key Stages 1, 2 and 3.

Organizational differences notwithstanding, the curriculum provision in each of the countries is broadly similar. All of them offer guidelines about the content and creation of schemes of work and all of them make reference to the enhancement of communication through the teaching of music and the transformation that it can bring to pupils' feelings, thoughts and actions.

All of the curriculum documents make reference to listening skills, the application of knowledge and understanding, performance skills, singing, playing, creating and composing. Furthermore, all of the documents link the study of music to an understanding of culture and diversity and in every case pupils are expected to appraise, respond to and review their own work and that of others.

Above all, the importance attached to music is indicated by the fact that the subject is a statutory entitlement for all pupils aged 5–14 in England, Wales, Scotland and Northern Ireland and must be made available within curriculum options beyond that age.

In reality, although there are differences between the four curriculum documents, for the most part they are differences of detail rather than fundamental philosophy. The English National Curriculum (National Curriculum for England, Programmes of Study) reflects views throughout the UK (and abroad) when it states:

> Music is a powerful, unique form of communication that can change the way pupils feel, think and act. It brings together intellect and feeling and enables personal expression, reflection and emotional development. As an integral part of culture, past and present, it helps pupils understand themselves and relate to others, forging important links between the home, school and the wider world. The teaching of music develops pupils' ability to listen and appreciate a wide variety of music and to make judgements about musical quality. It encourages active involvement in different forms of amateur music making (individual and communal) and develops a sense of group identity and togetherness. It also increases self-discipline and creativity, aesthetic sensitivity and fulfilment.

Further credence is given to this view by the Pre-school Music Association who state:

> ... movement and music greatly enhance the acquisition of language. (www.presma.org)

The work of Dr Alexandra Lamont, researcher and lecturer in Music Psychology at Keele University, Staffordshire (2003) led her to the conclusion that: 'Children who take part in music develop higher levels of social cohesion and understanding of themselves and others and the emotional aspect of musical activities seems to be beneficial for developing social skills like empathy.'

Such views are not unique to the UK. Research in the USA has come to the unequivocal conclusion that music education offers both economic and social benefits. In their 2002 report *Music Education Facts and Figures* the National Association for Music Education (USA) stated unequivocally that: 'Music programs in our schools help our kids and communities in real and substantial ways.'

The report continues by placing those benefits into four categories:

- success in society
- success in school
- success in developing intelligence
- success in life.

It cites extensive research to illustrate that success, including:

- 'Secondary students who participated in band or orchestra reported the lowest lifetime and current use of all substances [alcohol, tobacco, illicit drugs].' (Texas commission on drug and alcohol abuse report, January 1998)
- 'Many colleges view participation in the arts and music as a valuable experience that broadens students' understanding and appreciation of the world around them. It is also well known and widely recognized that the arts contribute significantly to children's intellectual development.' (*Getting Ready for College*

Early: A Handbook for Parents of Students in the Middle and Junior High School Years, US Department of Education, 1997)
- Physician and biologist Lewis Thomas studied the undergraduate majors of medical school applicants. He found that 66 per cent of music majors who applied to medical school were admitted, the highest percentage of any group. In addition, 44 per cent of biochemistry majors were admitted (as reported in *The Case for Music in the Schools*, Phi Delta Kappa, February 1994).
- Students in two Rhode Island elementary schools who were given an enriched, sequential, skill-building music program showed marked improvement in reading and math skills. Students in the enriched program who had started out behind the control group caught up to statistical equality in reading, and pulled ahead in math. (Gardiner, Fox, Jeffrey and Knowles, as reported in *Nature*, May 23, 1996)
- 'Music is about communication, creativity, and cooperation, and, by studying music in school, students have the opportunity to build on these skills, enrich their lives, and experience the world from a new perspective.' (Bill Clinton, former President, USA)

However, while those committed to the teaching of music in schools and conscious of its value may well welcome such statements and research findings they are, nevertheless, faced with a dichotomy when attempting to demonstrate the value of the subject within the curriculum, particularly if too great an emphasis is placed upon music's importance to pupils' academic performance in other curriculum areas.

How do we justify music?

There are those who would say that this is a question that we shouldn't need to ask. Music, they would say, justifies itself by its beauty, by the fact that it has an importance in every culture, by the fact that it moves the spirit and changes lives. While all of this is true teachers live, for better or for worse, in a rather more practical world where outcomes and success have to be seen to be believed. It is no coincidence that when the National Curriculum was being developed throughout the UK the last guidelines to be published were for those practical arts subjects, music among them, that are so hard to assess objectively. Since accountability remains one of the main platforms of any National Curriculum it is hardly surprising that music sometimes struggles to achieve a central role.

One of the perennial problems faced by music is that it is regarded a 'the icing on the cake', a minority 'hobby' subject which, although desirable is not particularly essential. Indeed, in the UK and arguably elsewhere, notwithstanding music's inclusion in the National Curriculum it could be argued that the very nature of its inclusion and the structure of the National Curriculum have, in part at least, contributed to its marginality.

By having subjects at its core and by making those subjects central to the system of SATs and school assessment there is, by implication, a hierarchy within the curriculum. That hierarchy, though by no means formal or official, is nevertheless perceived by teachers, parents and pupils alike. In their work in the UK for the National Foundation for Educational Research (NFER) *Pupils' Experiences and Perceptions of The National Curriculum and Assessment* (Final Report, 2006), Pippa Lord and Megan Jones concluded the following: 'Learners tend to have a narrow view of the relevance of the curriculum, associated with perceived subject status, assessment and "getting grades" (that is, implicit messages permeate pupils' views). Real-life connections, vocational and practical application are valued by pupils.'

It is through the recognition of these perceptions, and given the research we can hardly ignore them, that the dichotomy arises. If we seek to justify music by pointing out its undoubted value to other areas of the curriculum we are in danger of reinforcing the perceived hierarchy. If, on the other hand, we fail to make the connections then we are only telling half the story and doing an injustice to the subject that we are seeking to promote.

Fortunately there is a solution and thankfully it is a straightforward one. To do music justice we must tell the whole story and the last sentence of the NFER quote above gives us the necessary guidance. If 'real-life connections ... and practical application ...' are valued by pupils then that should be our starting point. Music does support other areas of the curriculum; we cannot escape that fact. However, in this case what is really important is the emphasis we place upon this information. We are only in danger of diminishing the role of music if we fail to make it clear that that role is central. International research has proved that music adds value in major ways to the learning and engagement of pupils. If the curriculum is to be balanced and we are to achieve maximum benefit for learners it is not enough to say, in an almost apologetic manner, it might be quite good if music was available. What we must say, because it is the truth, is that if we are to do the best for our children it is *vital* that music plays a part and we are morally obliged to create a curriculum that makes that opportunity available. Once we are clear in our minds about this we can begin to plan music provision from a point of strength and the claims that we make about the intrinsic value of music and its ability to enrich the lives of our pupils, rather than making our case more nebulous, actually give it more strength.

As the National Curriculum in the UK has evolved there has been a renewed recognition of the importance of the arts, thematic teaching and so on and this has been embodied, at primary level at least, in the documents relating to *Excellence and Enjoyment*, which will be dealt with in a later chapter. Additionally there is also a sense, promoted by strategies such as Ofsted's self-assessment review process, that the professional judgement of teachers is once more gaining respect. If this is the case, and it certainly seems to be, then teachers must seize the opportunity to shape the curriculum by ensuring that it serves the needs of pupils. They can only achieve this by ensuring a balanced curriculum that recognizes the importance of music in the education of our children.

The music manifesto

The British government launched the 'music manifesto' in 2004 and similar initiatives were introduced in Australia, New

Zealand, and large parts of the USA at around the same time. The British manifesto declared that it would:

- Act as a statement of common intent that helps align currently disparate activity.
- Set out a shared agenda for future planning, because we know that real progress depends on action by all of us.
- Make it easier for more organizations and individuals to see how they can contribute to music education.
- Guide government's own commitment.
- Call on the wider community, in the public, private and community sectors, to join us in enriching the lives of schoolchildren.

A closer examination of these statements reveals that the manifesto has five key aims and that each of those aims is supported by suggested strategies intended to improve music provision for our young people.

1) To provide every young person with first access to a range of music experiences:
- Every primary school child should have free or cheap instrumental tuition. 'Wider Opportunities' provision is an ideal way of achieving this (see Chapter 2, page 32).
- All children, including those with special needs, should receive teaching in general musicianship and should be able to experience a range of high quality performances.
- All music leaders, both inside and outside educational establishments, should be able to broaden the range of skills they can offer.
- Teaching methods, genres and activities should be varied both within school music lessons and in extra-curricular activities.
- Links should be made between schools, LEA's, LEA music services, musicians in the community and the music industry to widen provision.

2) Provide more opportunities for young people to deepen and broaden their musical interests and skills:

11

- Encourage the good delivery of secondary music education progressing from new initiatives in primary education.
- Have centres of excellence in music, for example existing arts colleges or higher education establishments.
- Enable young people to record and promote their own compositions with opportunities for live performances.
- Use ICT with music in more places.
- Strengthen the connection between young people's music in and out of school and identify positive role models (see 'Musical Futures', pages 37–8).
- Think creatively about improving the access young people have to resources, such as space and equipment in their local area.
- Inform young people of opportunities available to develop their involvement in music, including careers advice.
- Improve access to appropriate music qualifications.

3) Identify and nurture our most talented young musicians:
- Develop talent in young people who aspire to a career in music by providing access to high-level instrumental tuition and opportunities in the region or further away if appropriate.
- Explore the possibility of apprenticeships in the music industry and professional organizations.
- Develop increased links between schools, specialist music schools, conservatoires, FE and HE establishments to enable young people to develop skills relevant to professions.

4) Develop a world-class workforce in music education:
- Provide high quality continuing professional development to people who deliver music education.
- Provide young people with a variety of educators and encourage them to take careers advice.
- Teachers to forge links with other schools and professionals.
- Support for teachers using ICT with music in the classroom.
- Good practice to be shared through local clusters.
- Encouragement of musicians and composers to pass on skills through music education.
- Accredited qualification given for a variety of types of musical expertise.

- Joint training and planning for people who deliver music education both in and out of schools.

5) Improve the support and structures for young people's making music:
- Research the support needed for all types of music making by young people and develop existing support appropriately.
- Encourage the sources of support to liaise.
- Recognize and use private, independent and voluntary organizations who contribute to music education.
- Develop specific activities linked to the five priorities to build cross-sector support.

The manifesto is intended to cover activities for the next three to five years. There have been over 1,400 signatories to the manifesto who are committed to delivering wide ranging musical experiences to young people. Numerous individuals and organizations have made pledges of practical activities and resources to support the aims of the manifesto.

Following the launch of the manifesto, a number of projects were initiated. In November 2005 the 'pathfinder' projects were announced. This involved the use of three leading music organizations or 'pathfinders': The Hallé Orchestra and Manchester consortium, The Roundhouse and The Sage Gateshead. The pathfinders were given £2 million to develop projects that supported the aims of the manifesto and tested models of music provision that could then be developed around the country.

The three pathfinders took on different aims. The Manchester pathfinder concentrated on aim five of the manifesto – improving the support structures for young peoples' music making. They developed links between local music providers. Naomi Elliott-Newman, the coordinator, commented that projects had led to 'greatly enhanced working relationship and an awareness of the region'. One result of their work has been the sharing of good practice between local education authorities. The idea of Manchester's 'Singing School' (see Chapter 2, page 33) has been adopted by Salford schools. Manchester's schools have adopted the idea of 'satellite choirs', which Salford schools have been using for some time. This involves the grouping of several local school choirs to form a larger choir. These satellite choirs have gone on to perform alongside the Hallé Orchestra at the Bridgewater Hall.

The second music manifesto report was published in 2006 and recommended the formation of local hubs, which bring together music educators. Singing was recommended as a priority as 'the most direct route to providing a music-making experience for all children and young people'. The 2012 Olympic Games were suggested as a realistic goal.

The following steps were proposed to government and manifesto signatories:

1. Confirm the music standards fund until 2011 to enable music services to participate fully in strengthening and improving music education provision.
2. Commission a series of pilot projects to test the viability and key principles of music education hubs and school music federations in 2007/8 with a view to national implementation by 2011.
3. Carry out an urgent review to identify sustainable funding for community musicians while music education hubs are being established.
4. Implement a national campaign to provide singing for all early years and primary children by 2012, with a significant singing element in the cultural programme of the Olympic Games.
5. Introduce a musical passport scheme to enable young people to record and gain recognition for their individual musical achievements.
6. Build on the opportunities offered by such initiatives as the new creative diploma, Musical Futures and the Key Stage 2 music entitlement to extend the music offer to every young person with a particular focus on those who are vulnerable and marginalized.
7. Implement a programme of professional development for music educators with a focus on singing within early and primary years settings and the curriculum for the new creative diploma.

The then Education Secretary, Alan Johnson, responded to this with a number of plans including:

- the appointment of Howard Goodall as a 'singing ambassador' to lead a campaign for singing in primary schools
- a national songbook to use in schools including a variety of genres
- choir schools to provide increased outreach in their locality
- increased provision of 'Music Start'.

'Music Start' is an initiative developed by Youth Music to encourage music making for 2–5 year olds. The extra funding will be used to develop a pack for parents containing a CD and some percussion instruments to use with their child. Since 1999, more than £500 million has been invested in music education by the Department for Education and Skills (DfES), with a further £95 million designated for 2007/2008.

2

PRIMARY AND
SECONDARY
EDUCATION

Educational stages

Primary or elementary education consists of infant schools for ages 5–7 and junior schools for ages 7–11. Some infant and junior age groups combine in one school. The infant age group is made up of three year groups (Reception, Years 1 and 2). The junior age group consists of four year groups (Years 3–6). Some primary schools also have a nursery attached. This caters for children after their third birthday.

Primary education encompasses three stages: Foundation stage is for children aged 3–5 (nursery and Reception); Key Stage 1 covers the remaining infant age group (Years 1 and 2); and Key Stage 2 covers the junior age group (Years 3–6).

Some areas have middle schools. These act as a bridge between primary and secondary education and usually cover Years 5–8/9.

Secondary education caters for children aged between 11 and 18 and is made up of two compulsory stages and one optional. Key Stage 3 consists of Years 7–9 (age 11–14); Key Stage 4 consists of Years 10 and 11 (age 14–16); and Key Stage 5 consists of Years 12 and 13 (age 16–18/19). Compulsory education finishes at the end of Year 11 and pupils are able to continue into sixth form education if they choose. Many schools have their own sixth form but there are also separate sixth form colleges available.

The curriculum

Foundation stage

Curriculum guidelines were issued to all nurseries and schools in May 2000. These set out six areas of learning to form the curriculum. Each area has its own early learning goals. Music comes under the learning area of creative development and the goals can be found at www.underfives.co.uk/elg.html.

At the end of the Reception year, teachers are required to complete a Foundation stage profile for every child. This is a

17

record of progress and learning needs based on observations and assessments in each of the six learning areas. QCA report in the 2004/5 annual report on curriculum and assessment: 'Teachers and practitioners in the Foundation stage continue to emphasize creative development through the arts, including music, as they are seen to be a way of stimulating and improving learning in all areas of the Foundation stage curriculum. The arts can make a difference to pupils' well-being, through lifting their spirits and helping them express themselves.'

Key Stages 1, 2 and 3

The aim and purpose of music education at Key Stages 1, 2 and 3 are broadly the same. By engaging pupils in making and responding to music, music education offers opportunities for them to:

- Develop their understanding and appreciation of a wide range of music, extend their own interests and increase their ability to make judgements about music quality.
- Acquire the knowledge, skills and understanding needed to make music, for example in community music making, and, where appropriate, to follow a music-related career.
- Develop the skills, attitudes and attributes that can support learning in other subject areas and are needed for employment and life, for example listening skills, concentration, creativity, intuition, aesthetic sensitivity, perseverance, self-confidence and sensitivity towards others.

Key Stages 1–3 have a 'programme of study' (PoS). These set out what pupils should be taught and provide the basis for planning schemes of work. This is split into four sections:

- controlling sounds through singing and playing – performing skills
- creating and developing musical ideas – composing skills
- responding and reviewing – appraising skills
- listening, and applying knowledge and understanding.

Each of these sections of the PoS sets out the requirements to be taught:

- knowledge, skills and understanding
- breadth of study.

Performing, composing and appraising are interrelated and should be developed in all activities. These skills should also be developed through the application of listening skills as well as knowledge and understanding of music.

In particular, pupils should acquire and apply knowledge and understanding of:

- how music is constructed, for example the use of musical elements and devices
- how music is produced, for example the use of instruments, ICT, musical processes and procedures, including relevant symbols and notations
- how music is influenced by time and place, for example the effect of the occasion, purpose or venue.

The DfES has created guidance for parents in the form of a website 'The Learning Journey' (www.parentscentre.gov.uk/learningjourneys). This provides information about what is covered in school and how parents can help at home. Given the wealth of information offered on the site teachers may well find it advantageous to be familiar with it in the event that parents may wish to discuss it in connection with their child's learning.

Schemes of work

Key Stages 1 and 2

QCA provide a full exemplar scheme of work for Key Stages 1 and 2 (www.standards.dfes.gov.uk/schemes2/music/). This is not compulsory and teachers are able to choose to use as much or little as they deem suitable for their school. The scheme comprises of 21 units that can be adapted to suit the needs of particular schools. In a 2004/5 survey, QCA reported that 64 per cent of schools had used these schemes. QCA also give guidance on constructing a scheme of work for teachers who wish to create their own schemes.

Other resources are available for teachers such as 'Music Express' (see www.acblack.com/musicexpress/). This is a ready-made complete scheme for primary schools. It contains photo-copiable resources and is designed to be used by non-music specialists. The scheme can be bought with 'eLearning Credits' (see page 27).

Key Stage 3

The DfES standards site provides an example scheme of work for teachers comprising of 15 units – www.standards.dfes.gov.uk/schemes2/secondary_music/. Each unit is designed to last between 5–14 hours. QCA believe that 58 per cent of teachers use this scheme in its entirety.

The scheme is not statutory and is intended to serve as an example of how the programmes of study can be used to devise projects throughout the year. Teachers are encouraged to use as much or as little of the scheme as they judge appropriate. The units are explained in great detail so that teachers can apply the same approach to their own schemes if they wish. The section 'Principles for constructing a scheme of work' is particularly useful for teachers who want to assess or devise their own scheme of work.

Another popular package is 'New Music Matters' published by Heinemann, who claim that this is used by over 70 per cent of teachers in the UK at KS3. This is a self-contained scheme and consists of a pupil book, teacher's resource pack, an audio CD and CD-ROM for each of Years 7, 8 and 9.

Although ready-made schemes are extremely useful, many teachers create original projects according to their own enthu-siasms and areas of expertise. These can be tailored to the needs of the pupils within the school.

Assessment

Attainment targets for music are divided into eight levels. Each level describes different degrees of knowledge, skills and understanding so the teacher can assess where individual pupils are at the end of a key stage. The levels can be found at www.nc.uk.net/nc/contents/Mu—ATT.html.

By the end of Key Stage 1 most pupils should have attained level 2. They will have 'recognized and explored how sounds can be organized'. Higher achievers will reach level 3 and exceptional pupils will reach level 4. By the end of Key Stage 2 most pupils should have attained level 4. They will have 'identified and explored the relationship between sounds and how music reflects different intentions'. Higher achievers will reach level 5 and exceptional pupils will reach level 6.

KS3 children are expected to work within levels 3 to 7, with the expected attainment of the majority being levels 5/6 by the end of Year 9. Higher-achieving children will reach level 7 and a few of exceptional achievement will reach level 8.

At the end of each Key Stage, pupils take National Curriculum tests. For Key Stage 1 these are in English and maths. At the end of Key Stage 2, pupils are tested in English, maths and science. At the end of a Key Stage, teachers should judge which level description best fits the pupil's performance. The use of levels in music is not statutory for primary schools and there is variable use of them by KS1 and KS2 teachers.

One of the problems is the lack of confidence in non-specialist primary teachers. In 2004 QCA reported that: 'Where there is effective teaching, children in Years 1 to 6 can easily achieve the levels intended, but where teachers have had little training in music the levels become much more challenging.' This can pose a problem for music teachers at secondary level who rarely receive useful information regarding the individual abilities in music. 'There is very limited use of transfer data between Key Stages. Secondary teachers comment on the lack of information from primary schools, in particular information about the development of musical skills, knowledge and understanding.' Some schools do however liaise well and involve secondary music staff in Year 6 projects. Such projects 'have a positive impact on pupils' experience of transition from Key Stage 2 to Key Stage 3'. QCA acknowledge that there is a need for a form of record, which is relevant and easy to use for transfer to secondary school.

Teachers are required to give each Year 9 pupil a level at the end of the year and this is sent to the National Assessment Agency. Guidance is provided through the 'National Curriculum in Action' website and CD-ROM, which has been sent to all schools and LEA's – see www.ncaction.org.uk/subjects/music/. This demonstrates standards of students' work within and across different Key Stages; the translation of the programmes of study into useable activities; and how ICT can be used within music. The examples come from a broad variety of pupils, contexts and schools. This excellent resource gives detailed examples of students achieving each of the levels, advises teachers how to make a judgement at the end of a Key Stage and how to recognize progression.

The QCA site uses a variety of formats to present the examples and to give as clear a picture as possible of the process within the classroom:

- audio excerpts of pupils' performances, compositions and commentaries
- pupils' written responses
- transcripts of discussion
- visual material of musical scores
- pictures of pupils working
- visual examples of teaching material used.

The QCA 2004 report on *Curriculum and Assessment* comments that teachers do not make adequate use of the available resources – only a small proportion of teachers are aware of their existence and an even smaller proportion actually use them (less than a quarter). Teachers who make use of the site comment that it is very helpful and say that it 'translates what's on paper to a real situation that I can apply to my own classroom'.

Ofsted (2004) report that assessment of music is weak in Key Stage 3 and pupils are not often encouraged to assess their own work. They state that: 'Too often, particularly in Key Stage 3, pupils' work is assessed at the end of a series of lessons, with an emphasis on what has been produced, usually a composition or a performance. Often this does not take proper account of how pupils have acquired, developed and applied musical skills.'

This is not the case in all schools however. Ofsted also note that: 'Some schools are now very successful in assessment of large groups and practical workshops, which are typical in Key Stage 3, when pupils themselves are taught how to be critical and evaluative of their own and each others' work. Pupils in Years 7 to 9 can review, edit and evaluate their work when they receive clear guidance about the purpose of topics and tasks.'

Many teachers rewrite the attainment targets so that they can be more easily understood by students. Some even relate the targets to specific units of work so that the students have a clearer idea of expectations for each topic.

Assessing an individual student's musical experience of a project needs to be more than just assessing an outcome. The often complicated and multi-layered process of reaching the end product should also be taken into consideration. Ofsted agree that teachers 'need systems and procedures that capture and store what is important in music, not merely that which is measurable'. This may explain why some teachers assess 'by instinct' rather than by evidence at the end of a unit.

One of the main problems for secondary teachers is the lack of time. Most Key Stage 3 music lessons last for an hour and teachers usually only see classes once a week. The prospect of managing the assessment of perhaps over 500 students is a mammoth task for anyone.

ICT

ICT can have a huge impact in music teaching at all stages. QCA report that: 'Boys, in particular, respond well to the use of ICT in music.' QCA suggest that ICT can help pupils in the following ways:

- make and explore sounds
- record for different purposes
- structure music
- interact with different information sources
- perform and compose music
- understand musical processes.

Key Stages 1 and 2

There is no statutory requirement to use ICT in music at Key Stage 1. This is not to say that it can't be used to good effect – QCA suggest that pupils could use computer software that enables them to explore sounds in composition. Also pupils could record work that can then be evaluated and refined at a later date.

QCA recommend the following equipment for Key Stage 1:

- tape recorder with counter
- sound-processing toys capable of producing a range of effects transforming the voice to sound like a robot, ghost, cartoon character, and so on
- keyboard with a selection of voices
- multimedia PC with soundcard and speakers
- focused activity software such as pitch and rhythm games
- simple pattern sequencing software.

At Key Stage 2 QCA state that: 'Pupils should be taught the knowledge, skills and understanding through using ICT to capture, change and combine sounds.' They recommend the following equipment to assist learning at Key Stage 2:

- digital effects units
- MIDI keyboard featuring a wide range of preset sounds
- stereo tape recorder with microphone and line inputs
- software for recording and processing sound
- software for exploring style and structure
- simple sequencing software.

They also recommend software and hardware to develop pupils' work:

- MIDI keyboard featuring a facility to make alterations to sounds; recording and playback of several parts; limited sound sampling; disk drive
- minidisc recorder
- creative mixing software.

Programmes such as 'Compose World Play' for Foundation–Key Stage 2 and 'Compose World Create' for Key Stages 1 and 2 allow pupils to manipulate pre-recorded ideas (see www.espmusic.co.uk).

Ofsted (2004) reported on the benefit of interactive whiteboards when demonstrating new work to pupils. They also comment on good use of pre-recorded backing tracks and software enabling pupils to explore sound and structure in music. They comment on the problem of not allowing enough time for pupils to explore resources: 'When selections are made too quickly, the outcomes are often superficial and easily forgotten. Allowing pupils time to choose sound sources, then organize them in a musical structure, can promote rapid progress.' Ofsted also comment on the reliable way ICT can be used to save pupil's work for evaluation.

Key Stages 3–5

The National Curriculum states that students should use information and communication technology (ICT) to 'create, manipulate and refine sounds' at KS3. They should 'identify the use of ICT in selected genres, styles and traditions' and also the 'impact of ICT'. ICT can be an invaluable learning tool in music and its use can be applied across all aspects of music. Ofsted (2004) report that: 'When given sustained opportunities for exploring and using music technologies, pupils acquire and develop skills, often using them with individuality and flair.'

Backing tracks in the form of CDs or MIDI files on a computer can be an excellent aid for performing. Students can use them to improvise and as a starting point for composing melodies. If MIDI files are used, different parts of the backing can be muted so students could, for example, play chords or a percussion part and group-work can easily be developed.

Students enjoy having their work recorded and it acts as an added incentive to produce a polished performance within the given time. Tape recorders, minidisc recorders or computers can be used to record students and the recordings can then be used for student and teacher assessment.

Computers with a general MIDI sound source can be linked to a MIDI keyboard and used with sequencing software such as Cubase to explore the interaction of sounds and layered textures. Students can create multi-track recordings and can manipulate them by, for example, putting them in time or remixing them. The compositional possibilities are endless – teachers can create templates for students to work from and there are many products available to use within the classroom.

Heinemann publish a CD-ROM entitled 'ICT activities in Music', which contains a variety of useful activities for use across the music curriculum.

'Musition 3' from Sibelius is an interactive music theory CD-ROM which covers theory from the basics up to GCSE level and beyond. Examples of activities include: 'Tap a rhythm with the space bar ... identify pitches on treble, bass and C-clefs ... identify key signatures, chords and inversions.' This excellent resource also covers popular music theory such as chord symbol notation – see www.sibelius.com/products/musition.

'Sibelius Instruments' is a complete and interactive guide to the orchestra, which allows students to explore individual instruments, ensembles and repertoire among many other features – see www.sibelius.com/products/instruments. The internet has many useful sites such as the BBC music learning site which can support research and teaching – see www.bbc.co.uk/music/learning. The Associated Board of the Royal School of Music (ABRSM) have created a fantastic interactive website, 'Soundjunction' – www.soundjunction.org. This innovative resource allows students to 'listen, explore, discover and create'. The Department for Culture, Media and Sport report that: 'The website offers access to a range of exclusive musical experiences that promote a deep appreciation of the connections and distinctions between different cultures' musical methods and forms.' Users can deconstruct and re-assemble pieces of music into their own unique composition. There are tips from professional musicians and footage of performances.

All schools now have eLCs or eLearning Credits. This is money set aside for schools to spend on multimedia resources. These resources can be obtained from the website www.curriculumon-line.gov.uk. There are hundreds of music resources covering the entire curriculum.

Increasingly, schools are gaining more ICT equipment for music and some schools have fully equipped rooms where KS3 classes can work in pairs on computers with headphones. It is extremely useful to have a teacher computer, which can be linked to a data projector or interactive whiteboard so that onscreen demonstrations can be shared with a whole class. Some schools even have the teacher's computer set up with a system that can access any of the computers in the class during the lesson so the teacher can hear and see what the students are doing from their own computer and talk to the students through their headphones with a microphone.

The extent to which technology is used within KS3 music can often be dependent upon the knowledge and skills of the head of music. Shortage of ICT equipment and lack of facilities is usually the main obstacle in the use of ICT in music. Some local authorities provide good advice and support for teachers wishing to develop their skills and there are several training courses available throughout the year. Even one dedicated computer for music can be used to great effect in the classroom – the Ofsted 2004 report on ICT in secondary music contains examples of how one or a few computers can be successfully used in KS3 lessons.

QCA recommend the following equipment to assist learning at Key Stage 3:

- digital effects units with decent quality microphones and amplification
- computers with high quality soundcards and in sufficient

quantity to enable all students in a class to work in pairs at the same time
- music software specifically designed for exploring structures and styles
- sequencing software
- MIDI keyboards
- sampling and processing software
- 8- or 16-channel mixer linked to one computer and digital effects unit
- classroom-based PA system (linked to the mixer).

They also recommend the following software and hardware:

- music notation software
- four-track tape recorders
- DJ turntables or mixing devices
- innovative sound manipulation and control tools
- karaoke player (hardware or software based)
- CD-writer
- minidisc recorder with stereo microphone
- additional keyboards/synthesizers with extended features
- advanced software-based sampler and editor
- interactive whiteboard or digital projector
- internet links in the music classroom.

There are several good suppliers of educational resources – Music Village and Dolphin Music are both excellent. Music retailers such as Dawsons have educational departments and are always keen to forge links with local schools.

Peripatetic music

The case studies section on Shropshire (see Chapter 9) highlights how an LEA music service can provide an excellent package to its schools. Many schools employ the local authority music service to cater for students wishing to learn a musical instrument. In 2004 Ofsted reviewed the provision of music services in 15 local authorities. They reported a decline in the continuation of tuition throughout KS3 and KS4. Gender stereotyping was noted as an issue with girls, for example being much more likely to learn the flute than boys. A bias towards upper-pitched instruments in brass, strings and woodwind was also noted. These instruments are more plentiful due to their size and cost.

Most schools require students to come out of another lesson to attend their instrumental lesson and this can sometimes be a contentious issue with other subject staff. Some teachers have commented that other members of staff have, on occasion, refused to let students out of their lessons to attend an instrumental lesson, which had already been paid for by parents. One head of music commented: 'I certainly had many more problems with staff at schools where lessons were free.' Heads of music need to ensure that all other members of staff are aware of the timetabling issues for instrumental lessons and accept that it is sometimes necessary for students to miss part of a lesson. There should be an agreement that students catch up any work missed and the timetable should be rotated wherever possible to avoid hitting the same lesson every week. If all members of staff are made aware of the benefits that music making can bring to an individual and indeed a school, resistance is likely to be less.

The cost of peripatetic lessons can greatly vary between areas. Some music authorities give schools an allocation of free lesson time and any extra lesson cost is divided by the total number of pupils. In other areas parents have to pay the entire cost themselves.

Many music retailers offer good rates for the loan of instrument to students where the rental cost can be redeemed against the cost of the instrument if it is purchased.

Primary school issues

Primary National Strategy – 'Excellence and Enjoyment'

In 2003 the Primary National Strategy was introduced in the *Excellence and Enjoyment* paper. This built on the Literacy and

Numeracy Strategy already in place and extended similar support and guidelines to other subjects – modern foreign languages, PE and music.

The aim of the Primary Strategy is to combine excellent teaching with enjoyment of learning. Schools are encouraged to reflect the context of their school and pupils through choices they make within the curriculum. The strategy from the DfES states that schools will:

- develop the distinctive character of the school, building on existing strengths (for example sport or music) or working closely with the community
- take ownership of the curriculum
- be creative and innovative in how they teach and in how they run the school
- use tests, targets and tables to help every child develop their potential and measure school performance.

In the 2006 report *The Changing Role of the Music Coordinator*, Stuart Button and Alison Potter comment: 'Without the intervention of a music coordinator many generalist teachers will be unable to realize some of the objectives set out in the primary strategy document with respect to music.'

The primary music coordinator

Many teachers believe that music is one of the most difficult Foundation subjects to cover at Key Stages 1 and 2. For this reason, most primary schools have a music coordinator. This is a general primary teacher who takes on additional responsibility. Not all music coordinators have received training in their pre-teaching studies for this role and some simply 'have an interest in music'. Many primary teachers do not feel equipped to deliver an adequate music curriculum. The EMI Sound Foundation carried out research in April 2007 for the music manifesto. They commented that: 'As well as receiving inadequate training in music prior to commencing their careers, the teachers participating in the research also felt that in-service training they had received in music had been short and had minimal impact on their teaching.'

The QCA schemes can be difficult for non-specialists to understand and teachers can feel overwhelmed at the breadth and depth they are required to cover. A music coordinator commented: 'Nearly everyone in the school lacks confidence in teaching music and I think they rely on the scheme. The Year 5 and 6 teachers say that they don't understand the scheme at that level but I haven't had the time to sort it out.' In some schools, the music coordinator delivers music lessons rather than supporting other teachers to develop their own abilities in music teaching.

Resources in the form of time and suitable materials need to be made available to all schools. The EMI research reported that: 'There is a clear need for additional training in music for primary school teachers and that the issue of music resources needs to be addressed.' QCA also reported in the 2004/5 report that progress was seen in schools where music coordinators had been given regular time to address their responsibilities. Some schools were limited in terms of resources because 'music is not seen as a priority'. Only 3 per cent of schools made music the main subject focus for curriculum development in 2005/6.

The success of music in the primary school is inextricably linked with the abilities and vision of the music coordinator and the importance of this role should not be underestimated. The music coordinator ideally needs to have subject specific qualifications in music. There is a shortage of eligible primary teachers for the role – the number of primary teacher job adverts that have 'an interest in music would be advantageous' tagged hopefully at the end is a reflection of this. The successful coordinator enables all staff to deliver music lessons through demonstration and support and ensures that music permeates more than just an allocated short slot every week. Some schools provide excellent provision for music by employing a part-time music specialist to deliver this aspect of the curriculum. Holy Trinity School in Littleborough, for example, have a part-time music specialist who delivers all of the music lessons throughout the school. She also runs several extra-curricular groups. In schools unable to recruit a suitably qualified music specialist, it is especially important that initiatives such as 'Wider Opportunities' are explored.

'Wider Opportunities'

The 'Wider Opportunities' government pledge is that all primary pupils should have the opportunity to learn a musical instrument.

In 2004 the *Tuning In* paper – an evaluation of pilot Wider Opportunity programmes – was released. These 13 pilot programmes gave KS2 pupils musical skills and experiences so that they could make an informed choice regarding which instrument they would like to learn. They then embarked on tuition for all interested pupils. Music services and freelance musicians were involved in the delivery of the programme. Training and support was given to all staff involved. In several of the pilot schools instrumental take up after the programme was 70–100 per cent. Good quality teaching and materials were, unsurprisingly, found to enthuse, inform and sustain commitment from pupils.

The feedback from the evaluation was extremely positive. Pupils who began specialist tuition in Year 4 or 5 had made enough progress at the end of Year 6 to remain committed and motivated to continuing tuition at secondary school.

Following the success of the pilot projects, the government allocated up to £31.5 million for local music services Wider Opportunities projects over 2006/7 and 2007/8. QCA comment on the success of the projects in the 2004/5 music report, particularly on improved attainment at Key Stage 2 and general cross-curricular motivation and improvements. 'Such reports support the assertion that music can make a significant contribution to the whole school, can help to increase pupils' concentration, motivation and sensitivity towards others, and can stimulate and support learning across the curriculum.'

Singing

In response to the music manifesto report *Making Every Child's Music Matter*, the government launched a new singing campaign in January 2007 headed by Howard Goodall. Ten million pounds has been allocated for this project, which is based in primary schools. Howard Goodall sums up why singing is so important in the music manifesto:

> Singing is as natural and enjoyable to human beings as laughing. It is easy and universal, bonding us first to our mothers and then to each other. It complements our grasp of language and communication and accelerates our learning processes. It does not belong exclusively to one culture or another and cannot be traced, like musical instruments, through some distant family tree back to one place, time or tribe. It is the cheapest form of musical expression and where most children's musical journey begins.

A national songbook is being developed, combining a variety of genres of music for use in primary schools. There are a number of choir schools in Britain – 44 at present. These are mainly fee-paying and are attached to cathedrals, churches and college chapels. The Choir Schools' Association say that: 'Pupils have unlimited access to first-class schooling and musical training, giving them an excellent start in life.'

Howard Goodall recommends that these schools extend their outreach to boost local singing: 'It is essential that the unique qualities and skills of the choir school tradition in our country are unlocked for all – it is equally essential that the choir schools are able to open up wider and wider constituencies for their recruitment.'

Manchester music service launched an initiative called the 'Singing School', which was intended to use singing across the curriculum for the purpose of learning and enjoyment. A book and CD were given to every school. These contained old and new songs and contained appropriate music for use during numeracy work for example. Teachers were given training on how to use the materials throughout the school day. The music manifesto reported that teachers noted 'marked improvements in pupils' learning and concentration'.

There is certainly not a lack of enthusiasm for singing in primary schools. In April 2007, the BBC launched a competition to find a school choir to take part in the final *Any Dream Will Do* TV programme. The website was inundated with entries – over 840 primary schools applied. The BBC commented on the 'passionate interest in the competition'. Andrew Lloyd Webber commented: 'The standard of entries has been exceptional and is a credit to the dedicated music staff at the hundreds of schools which entered. It is also extremely encouraging to see such talent and enthusiasm from the pupils.'

The benefits of music in primary schools

Music can have a profound impact on all schools, including primary schools. The 2002 investigation into arts-rich schools reported: 'Conversations with headteachers about the reasons for provision tended to reinforce the conclusion that schools invest in the arts because headteachers believe that achievement in the arts will have a positive effect on pupils' behaviour, self-esteem and, ultimately, on their achievement across the curriculum, not just in the arts.'

In one school studied, National Curriculum results in English, maths and science had improved by 20 per cent over the four years that arts became a priority. The 2005 Ofsted primary music report observed common features of schools with strengths in music. These can be summarized in the following points:

- Music is seen as a priority in the school and there is a commitment to creative development.
- Supportive management who allow the coordinator time to fulfil their role.
- Coordinators support class teachers by identifying and building upon their existing musical skills so that confidence is developed.
- Resources support and develop staff expertise. Professional development in music is given to all staff.
- Coordinators deliver some lessons that are followed up and consolidated by the class teacher.

- Schools use LEA support and all available existing resources to good effect. Teachers follow up new ideas and take ownership of them. Wider opportunities projects are integral in developing success in primary schools.
- Coordinators ensure that all staff are aware of inclusion.

Secondary school issues

Time

The *Dearing Report* (1996) recommended that students should receive 45 hours a year or 1 hour 15 minutes a week for music. Most music lessons last for an hour and students can often find this frustrating when working on practical tasks. Ofsted state that: 'Without sufficient time for pupils to explore and develop their ideas, progress will be slow.'

Key Stage 4 students often comment positively on the increased time allowance to develop ideas. QCA report that: 'Reducing the time for music lessons affects pupils' confidence, since they have less time for practical music-making.'

Homework

Considering the fact that many students spend much time out of school listening to, buying and increasingly making music, official homework is often an area of neglect. QCA comment that: 'Too often, activities in the classroom are repetitive or limited, so that pupils perceive music in school to be unrelated to the enthusiasm and commitment that derives from their experience of music in their private time.' Explicit connections between music in and out of school can often be made and opportunities to make music relevant to students' own experience can frequently be wasted, by giving homework for homework's sake. Homework that serves to consolidate learning or prepare students for the next lesson is effective and relevant to students. One head of music, who preferred not to be named commented: 'We rarely give homework as most of what we would need pupils to do would require a specific resource at home (for example a keyboard or music software). Where applicable, homework is given. For example pupils may keep a diary of their progress through a certain task, and set targets. In general this may only mean homework given in four or five lessons within any given year.'

Accommodation

Accommodation for secondary music is often problematic and is 'still unsatisfactory in one in four schools' according to Ofsted. The nature of the subject requires space to make noise and for groups to work without disturbing others. We have had groups of students working in the canteen, storerooms and even corridors in order to give them a space to work effectively as a group! A number of small practice rooms are needed in addition to classrooms. Groups of students work well independently in practice rooms during lessons and these rooms can be used by individuals or groups out of lesson time. If practice rooms are needed for whole days for peripatetic teaching, it is beneficial to have an even greater number of rooms. The Department of Education for Northern Ireland (DENI) website provides excellent guidelines for music department room planning.

The future of music education at Key Stage 3

Personalized learning or 'education tailored to the individual' was one of the proposals set out in the White Paper *Higher Standards, Better Schools For All: More Choice for Parents and Pupils* in 2005. The DfES reported that: 'We have dramatically expanded our knowledge about how different young people acquire knowledge and skills. Coupled with increased resources in our schools, a reformed school workforce and the greater availability of ICT, this gives teachers the opportunity to tailor lessons and support in schools to the individual needs of each pupil.'

Key Stage 3 students are the most likely age group for disengagement in school music. Only 8 per cent of students start to learn a new instrument during this time. Conversely, this is also the age when students develop strong interests in music out of school.

In 2005 Ofsted reported that: 'The greatest challenge in secondary music is to engage Key Stage 3 pupils in a curriculum that is motivating, challenging and relevant. Too often activities are repetitive or limited, so that pupils perceive music in school to be unrelated to the enthusiasm and commitment that derives from their experience of music in their private time.'

In her 2001 study, Dr Alexandra Lamont reports: 'Since the decline in musical engagement seems to take place on a slower timescale than that of school in general, there may be scope for interventions using music to work with vulnerable children as they move into and through the early years of secondary school.'

'Musical Futures' is a project from the Paul Hamlyn Foundation. It aims to devise 'new and imaginative ways of engaging young people, aged 11–19, in music activities'. The findings will then be used to inform the wider use of sustainable models. Musical Futures is based on the concept of personalized learning using methods modelled from pop musicians. This involved groups of pupils working on performance based projects using informal methods. Teachers and a range of outside musicians gave guidance to the pupils, who took on more responsibility in devising and appraising tasks. Although the genre of pop music was the starting point for projects, in some cases knowledge, skills and understanding were then applied to classical music.

Ofsted reported that the projects were well received in schools and that teachers were 'invigorated' by the opportunity to challenge established teaching methods. They commented that: 'Pupils' motivation increased significantly, which was having a marked positive impact on the whole school. A particular feature was how inclusive the project was: pupils responded positively to being treated equally as musicians.'

In conjunction with Musical Futures, a website 'NUMU' has been developed. This is a 'dedicated safe space for young people to showcase their music, meet others and learn new skills. It is designed to support the music curriculum across primary and secondary and integrates with the innovative learning approaches of Musical Futures'. Pupils are able to upload tracks, which can then be assessed by other members of the site. They can collaborate with members over the internet in a secure environment.

The national strategy for Key Stage 3 music is another optional initiative with the following aims and intentions:

- continuing professional development programme for teachers
- approach to planned learning for students at KS3 based on the development of their musical understanding through a practical engagement with music
- development of a range of teaching strategies to support that planned learning.

LEA's launched the strategy in January 2007 and are currently providing training for teachers. As of yet, the music strategy has not been published on the standards site. The implications of the national strategy are similar in many ways to those encompassed in Musical Futures and are an indication of the likely direction of secondary music teaching in the future. The document *Musical Futures and the Secondary National Strategy Key Stage 3 Music Programme* highlights the similarities.

Both approaches encourage:

- students to engage with music as a whole.

Both approaches emphasize:

- the importance of process to musical learning – how you learn being as important as what you learn
- that practical, creative engagement with music is essential to learning.

Both approaches also promote:

- students' modelling and leading learning in the classroom
- live performances and leadership in the classroom from external musicians

- students engaging with the raw materials and processes of music by analysing existing musical ideas and seeing how they can best be arranged or performed
- a breadth of musical learning, including a wide variety of genres and styles
- networking for teachers to enable effective pedagogical development.

The transfer from primary to secondary

There is a considerable amount of evidence to suggest that although younger children have very positive attitudes towards music, many pupils lose interest after the transition to KS3. This is despite music being taught as a discrete timetabled lesson at secondary school, whereas at primary school the provision is often more variable. QCA reported on the importance of transfer data in 2005 and the need for KS3 teachers receiving 'specific information about individual pupils' strengths, weaknesses and instrumental skills'. Some secondary schools have taken matters into their own hands as a head of music commented: 'One of my colleagues has been given extra responsibility for visiting our partner primary schools and at least keeping a record of gifted and talented musicians, instrument players, choir members, and so on.'

In the report *Understanding the Decline in Children's Music Participation following the Transition to Secondary School* (2001), the author Dr Susan O'Neill makes a number of recommendations:

1. 'Provide structured opportunities for young people which give them increasing choice, control, and responsibility for organising and developing their own musical involvement.' Pupils are often accustomed to having freedom within primary music lessons in choosing instruments and class groupings themselves. As they enter secondary school they become increasingly independent but in music lessons often find that they have less choice and more impositions than in KS2.

2. 'Provide young people with instruments that they associate with valued role models.'

    The recorder is one of the most common instruments encountered in Year 6 and 7. As students progress through KS3, adult role models are increasingly influential especially among boys. Students are not likely to find the prospect of playing instruments that they regard as being 'for children' very motivating.

3. 'Start learning to play an instrument younger, and at least one year before making the transition to secondary school.' This issue is being addressed through the 'Wider Opportunities' initiative (see page 32).

4. 'Help to establish within young people positive beliefs and values about musical involvement.'

    Teachers need to identify students who received instrumental tuition at primary school and encourage the continuation at secondary. Involvement in music should be promoted and celebrated within the culture of the school.

5. 'Provide young people with structured goals and appropriate challenges.' Students can be motivated by the deadline of an examination or assessment and make progress regardless of the result.

3
BEYOND KEY STAGE 3

GCSE

The year 2000 brought about important changes in the syllabus at GCSE level. New subject criteria were designed to ensure that specifications or syllabuses were built on the knowledge, understanding and skills established by the National Curriculum for England and Wales. The aims are very similar to those for Key Stage 3 (see Chapter 2, page 18).

- All specifications must give students opportunities to develop their understanding and appreciation of a range of different kinds of music, extending their own interests and increasing their ability to make judgements about musical quality.
- All specifications must give students opportunities to acquire the knowledge, skills and understanding needed to: make music, both individually and in groups; develop a lifelong interest in music, for example through community music making; progress to further study, for example A/AS level and other equivalent qualifications, and/or to follow a music-related career, where appropriate.
- All specifications must give students opportunities to develop broader life-skills and attributes including critical and creative thinking, aesthetic sensitivity and emotional and cultural development.

Assessment objectives

The programme of study used in Key Stage 3 is rewritten as three 'assessment objectives'. A specification must require candidates to demonstrate aural perception, musical knowledge and understanding and communication through:

1. AO1 singing and/or playing an individual part (that is, one that is not doubled). This could be a solo, accompanied or unaccompanied or an individual part in an ensemble with technical control, expression, interpretation and, where appropriate, a sense of ensemble (this could include

realization of own composition in the short course) – performing skills. In the full course at least one performance must include a significant part in an ensemble.

2. AO2 creating and developing musical ideas in relation to a given or chosen brief (in the short course this could include improvisation) – composing skills. The brief must describe the stimulus for the composition, provide a clear indication of the candidate's intentions and, for at least one composition, make connections with an area of study.

3. AO3 analysing and evaluating music using a musical terminology – appraising skills.

Again teachers are reminded that these objectives are inter-related and that 'connections should be made wherever possible in the assessment components'.

Specification content

The details given in the KS3 document concerning specific topics to cover are expanded. A specification must require candidates, through performing, composing and appraising, to develop aural perception and musical knowledge and understanding of:

1. The use of musical elements, devices, tonalities and structures.
2. The use of resources, conventions, processes and relevant notations including staff notation.
3. The contextual influences that affect the way music is created, performed and heard, for example the effect of different intentions, uses, venues, occasions, available resources and the cultural environment.

Areas of study

Performing, composing and appraising are related to each other through a range of areas of study. The areas cover classical music, popular music and world music. Each syllabus has its own areas of study although some are the same. Examples include dance music (OCR, AQA), music for special events/occasions (AQA, WJEC) and popular music in context (Edexcel).

Key skills

Key skills are the skills that will be required in the world of work and are important in many aspects of life. These include:

- communication
- application of number
- information and communication technology
- problem solving
- improving own learning and performance
- working with others.

Qualifications in key skills are available at different levels and pupils are given opportunities to use evidence for their assessment through all subjects, including GCSE music.

Syllabus choices

There are currently five providers of GCSE and A level music syllabuses: the Assessment and Qualifications Alliance (AQA); the Council for Curriculum, Examinations and Assessment (CCEA) – this is usually used in Northern Ireland; Edexcel; Oxford, Cambridge and RSA Examinations (OCR) and the Welsh Joint Education Committee (WJEC).

The syllabuses differ slightly in terms of assessment objective weightings. AQA award 33.3 per cent for each; CCEA and Edexcel award 30 per cent each to AO1 and AO2 and 40 per cent to AO3; OCR award 30–35 per cent for both AO1 and AO2 with 35 per cent for AO3; and WJEC award 30 per cent for AO1 and AO3 with 40 per cent for AO2.

Both AQA and OCR use the 'integrated assignment', which integrated all three of the assessment objectives.

All examination boards require teachers to internally assess approximately 50 per cent of the course AO1 and/or AO2.

Uptake and attitudes

According to the QCA, only 9 per cent of the English school population opted to study GCSE music in 2003. This placed it among the least popular subjects. While uptake has since increased slightly it is still a minority subject at GCSE.

During Year 9 GCSE option evenings many parents reveal their misconceptions about the subject by asking questions such as:

- 'My son is taking Grade 5 piano – is this equivalent to GCSE?'
- 'Can you still do A level music if you haven't done GCSE?'
- 'Do you think they might be better keeping it as a hobby?'

Some sixth form colleges require students to have achieved a Grade B at GCSE *and* to have Grade 5 theory in order to progress on to A level. The ABRSM examinations are, of course, an excellent route to take but should not be considered as a substitute for GCSE music. As discussed, composition and appraising skills make up approximately 70 per cent of the GCSE and these are not included in ABRSM examinations. Students can take the A level without having the GCSE but they are clearly at a disadvantage. ABRSM examinations Grades 6–8 are worth UCAS points when applying for higher education.

GCSE classes in the past were mainly filled with students who had learned an instrument for several years and already taken ABRSM examinations. As the gap between KS3 and KS4 was bridged with the revised GCSE curriculum in 2000, more students began to see GCSE music as a realistic option after Key Stage 3.

The latest Edexcel specification for GCSE music describes itself 'as an extension of classroom work done in Key Stage 3 of the National Curriculum, it caters for a wide spectrum of musical abilities and requirements'.

In some schools numbers have dramatically increased due to initiatives such as 'Musical Futures' (see Chapter 2, pages 37–8). Musical Futures report that: 'When questioned at the end of Years 7 and 8 in July 2006 the average percentage of students from two out of the three areas involved in the project intending to take GCSE music was 42.5 per cent.'

The implications of increased uptake

With coursework being such an important element of GCSE, it is important that students are able to receive appropriate guidance throughout the process from their teacher. One teacher (who preferred not to be named), commented: 'I can't get round all of the pupils in one lesson – it can take about 10 minutes to assess where a pupil's composition is up to and give advice.'

Space is also a problem for many teachers, as students need a space to work effectively on performing and composing. If students are working with headphones on a computer there are few problems, but if a class of 25 needs to split up to rehearse group performing in spaces where they are not disturbing others, noise and rooming can be problematic. Teachers often have to ensure that there are no peripatetic lessons on at the same time as GCSE classes because they usually need to use all of the practice rooms.

Moderation of coursework is extremely time consuming – as stated previously, this is approximately 50 per cent of the course. Ofsted (2006) reported: 'The main concern among teachers is about the assessment load and the effect this is having on the ability of teachers to take on larger classes.'

Class size is an issue in many schools – teachers of all subjects would undoubtedly wish for smaller classes wherever possible. The issues of noise, the need for working space and the individual attention needed by students makes this issue especially pertinent for music. The Department of Education for Northern Ireland recommend that 20 is the maximum number of students in a class at Key Stage 3, 15 at GCSE and 12 at A level.

Review of the GCSE music syllabuses and progression to A level

Overall, the impact of the 2000 curriculum changes has been well received by music teachers. The syllabuses are now much more accessible to all students who have progressed through Key Stage 3. The range of genres included in the syllabuses is large and not restricted to classical music, as in the past. Much of the course is practical and GCSE students are involved in performing and composing for at least 60 per cent of the course. The integration of the assessment objectives means that factual information and theoretical skills are related to practical activities.

However, some teachers say that the new syllabus has lost several features of their predecessors. QCA (2007) report:

> There is much less emphasis on musical literacy; several aspects of the performing component are affected: the minimum demand of pieces now needed to achieve the higher grades is very low; assessment via coursework has replaced the live concert environment for most candidates; and unprepared sight-reading and improvisation are no longer assessed; the move to short answer, structured and multiple choice questions means there are no opportunities for candidates to develop substantial essay-based answers requiring detailed knowledge of set works.

These losses have occurred as a result of making the course more accessible for students. As an example, a student who performs 'easier' level pieces in an Edexcel GCSE music examination gets their final mark scaled down to compensate for the 'easier' level. These pieces could be the equivalent of Grade 1 ABRSM. If the individual pieces were performed perfectly, they would gain 22 out of 25 or 88 per cent in performing. This would work out at as at least a Grade A in performing. Such a student would find the demands of performing far more difficult at AS level. AS and A2 music are suitable preparation for students wishing to progress onto a degree level course and their demands have remained appropriate for this purpose despite syllabus changes in 2000.

A level music

The design of A level music in England and Wales changed with the curriculum 2000 reforms. Assessment took the form of six units – three in the first year of study (AS music), and three in the second year of study (A2 music). This separation enabled students to gain an accredited qualification after a year, which could then be built upon to gain the A level with a further year of music.

The aims are a development of those at GCSE. AS and A level specifications in music should encourage students to:

- Extend the skills, knowledge and understanding needed to communicate through music and to take part in making music.
- Engage in and extend their appreciation of the diverse and dynamic heritage of music, promoting spiritual and cultural development.
- Develop particular strengths and interests encouraging life-long learning and providing access to music-related and other careers.
- Recognize the interdependence of musical skills, knowledge and understanding and the links between the activities of performing/realizing, composing and appraising.

According to the QCA (2006): 'AS and A level specifications should also encourage students to broaden experience, develop imagination, foster creativity and promote personal and social development.'

In addition, the A level specification should build upon and extend the skills, knowledge and understanding developed in the AS and serve as a foundation for further study in music.

Assessment objectives

The assessment objectives at AS and A2 are basically the same as GCSE:

1. AO1 performing – interpret musical ideas with technical and expressive control and a sense of style and awareness of occasion and/or ensemble.
2. AO2 composing – develop musical ideas with technical and expressive control making creative use of musical devices and conventions.
3. AO3 understanding – demonstrate understanding of, and comment perceptively on, the structural, expressive and contextual aspects of music.

All assessment objectives should assess aural perception skills and the application of knowledge and understanding.

At A2, all subjects should include synoptic assessment. In music students are required to:

-   make connections between different aspects of musical activities
-   apply the skills, knowledge and understanding described in the assessment objectives to unfamiliar music
-   demonstrate aural perception and aural discrimination.

Examples of this include:

-   analysing the musical characteristics of an unfamiliar piece in order to relate the music to a specific time and place
-   using knowledge of conventions to inform performance techniques
-   composing to a specific brief, which requires the use of specific musical features.

Music specification content

The AS and A level specifications are built on what students should have already covered in KS3 and GCSE music. AS and A level specifications should require candidates to develop aural perception skills and the ability to:

- Make expressive use of musical elements, structures and resources through interpreting musical ideas; creating and developing musical ideas using innovative and/or established musical techniques.
- Make critical judgements about the use of musical elements, structures and resources through analysing, evaluating and reflecting on own and others' work.

The expected level of performing is approximately Grade 5 ABRSM at AS level and Grade 6 at A2. Other examining bodies such as Trinity are also accepted at the same level.

Music areas of study

Students study in depth two contrasting areas of study at AS and A level – one of these must be from the 'Western classical' tradition. Breadth of understanding is gained through the placement of these areas within a broader context. Aspects of continuity and change are studied through examination of a selection of works. Musical theory skills are developed from GCSE.

At A2, candidates are required to increase depth of study in one of the areas selected at AS and to increase breadth of study by including a new area of study. Students are expected to use longer, essay style answers in the A2 written examination. The quality of written communication is assessed at AS and A2.

Uptake

As discussed previously, the large gap in difficulty makes AS level an unrealistic option for many students who have achieved well at GCSE. Numbers are again among the lowest subjects. According to Cambridge Assessment (2005), only 2 per cent of A level entries are for music.

Key skills

Again, all specifications provide opportunities for students to gain evidence for key skill assessment. The use of IT in music provides students with extensive opportunities to create and record evidence for their key skills portfolios.

A level music technology

Music technology consists of two units at AS and two units at A2. The aims of A level music technology are the same as those for A level music, as are the opportunities for using key skills. The assessment objectives are also the same with some additions:

1) AO4 – demonstrate effective use of music technology to capture, edit and produce musical outcomes.
2) AO5 – demonstrate understanding of and comment perceptively on the technical processes and principles that underpin effective use of music technology.

The inclusion of synoptic assessment is the same as for music. The information concerning specification content is also the same, with the omission of performing standards, which do not form part of the music technology course.

Music technology areas of study

Students study in depth two contrasting areas of study at AS and A level – one of these must reflect an historical and contextual aspect of music with technological relevance. Breadth of understanding is gained through the placement of these areas within a broader context. Musical theory skills are developed from GCSE, including relevant aspects of notation for music technology. Knowledge, understanding and specialist vocabulary are also related to the production, recording and editing of sound.

At A2, candidates are required to increase depth of study in one of the areas selected at AS and to increase breadth of study by including a new area of study. The quality of written communication is assessed at AS and A2.

Uptake

There have, as yet, been no official figures for the uptake of A level music technology. The last report by Cambridge Assessment covered the years 2001–2005 and did not include music technology. Secondary teachers report that uptake is good and the subject receives similar numbers, if not more, than for A level music. One secondary teacher commented 'numerous pupils, boys in particular, choose the course thinking that they will learn to use DJ decks and then drop it after about a week'.

The specification has many features in common with music A level. Students are required to have a good standard of musical literacy and all round musicianship. Some sixth forms require a Grade B or above in GCSE music, the ability to play an instrument and the ability to read music fluently. In 2005 Edexcel announced that they would be discontinuing the course. As the only provider of music technology A level this decision was met with uproar – teachers lobbied *The Times Educational* website and the decision was rescinded. Edexcel have recently released a draft version of the specification for 2010 so the future of the subject appears secure for now.

Vocational courses

There are other, more vocational, options available for students wishing to take this route. The BTEC First Certificate and Diploma in Performing Arts (music) is a 'NQF level 2' course. The National Qualifications Framework (NQF) sets out levels for different qualifications. GCSE is level 2 and A level is level 3. The BTEC first certificate is equivalent to two GCSEs and the diploma is equivalent to four GCSEs. These are designed to prepare young people for a career in music or progression onto further study.

The BTEC National Award in Music Performing or Composing is a level 3 course and equivalent to one A level.

All of these options are designed to give specialized work-related qualifications. The courses can be adapted to suit the nature of the students with some degree of choice in units.

'Access to music' provides a variety of vocational pop music based courses at different NQF levels.

Some universities do not accept BTEC qualifications for entry instead of A levels so this should be a consideration when students are making course choices.

4
THE
IMPORTANCE OF
MUSIC AND THE
CREATIVE
PROCESS

Music is a powerful, unique form of communication that can change the way pupils feel, think and act. It brings together intellect and feeling and enables personal expression, reflection and emotional development. As an integral part of culture, past and present, it helps pupils understand themselves and relate to others, forging important links between the home, school and the wider world. The teaching of music develops pupils' ability to listen and appreciate a wide variety of music and to make judgements about musical quality. It encourages active involvement in different forms of amateur music making, both individual and communal, developing a sense of group identity and togetherness. It also increases self-discipline and creativity, aesthetic sensitivity and fulfilment. (National Curriculum for England and Wales, online)

In 2000 a major review of the National Curriculum for England and Wales took place. As with any review there were numerous findings, some more significant than others. Perhaps most significant for teachers of the arts was that creativity was emphasized as an important aim and the then British Secretary of State for Education called upon the Qualifications and Curriculum Authority (QCA) to investigate how schools might best develop the creativity of their pupils through the National Curriculum. Throughout their investigations the QCA worked closely with teachers, gathering examples of pupils' work and good practice from every Key Stage and examining how existing schemes and lesson plans might be used or adapted to promote and develop creativity.

Not surprisingly a wealth of good practice was found within the creative curriculum and it is gratifying for teachers of music and other creative arts to know that their work is recognized and valued, particularly when the curriculum is under such pressure in terms of time and financial resources. Given this pressure the key question that those charged with delivering and supporting the arts must answer is: Why is creativity and in this particular case music, so important?

Motivating pupils

Sadly, despite the weight of research in its favour, there is a problem motivating students to carry on with the study of music. In England only 7 per cent choose to study it at GCSE and this problem is mirrored in other parts of the English-speaking world. Since educators fought so hard to ensure that music was retained within the curriculum it is, to say the least, a little alarming to discover that students are so eager to discontinue their studies.

Teachers might argue, sometimes with justification, that poor provision in the early years, restricted access to the subject and disadvantageous option systems must take some of the blame but unfortunately explaining the problems does nothing to address them. What teachers need to do is to examine what it is that makes them believe in music and armed with that information they must then set about winning over colleagues, parents and students.

Why is music so important?

'Music is the manifestation of the human spirit, similar to language. Its greatest practitioners have conveyed to mankind things not possible to say in any other language. If we do not want these things to remain dead treasures, we must do our utmost to make the greatest possible number of people understand their idiom.' (Zoltán Kodály, musician, composer and educational theorist.)

Kodály was in no doubt about the benefits that music could bring to peoples' lives and in particular how it can be used to enhance learning. A wide body of opinion and considerable research support this view claiming that music:

- integrates the concrete and the conceptual
- develops both independent thought and collaboration
- develops higher-order thinking skills including analysis and synthesis
- develops skills for problem solving
- provides opportunities for self-expression giving a voice to thoughts and feelings

- cuts across racial, social and cultural boundaries
- gives the opportunity to explore content, process and product
- provides reward, feedback and opportunity for reflection and evaluation
- improves academic achievement by developing thinking skills.

On the basis of this list alone it would be possible to create a fairly formidable case for music and its inclusion in the curriculum, but in addition to this there are other claims that merit examination and that make the case for music even stronger. On 20 September 2006 *The Times* newspaper published an article by Mark Henderson reporting that: 'Music lessons may improve memory and learning ability in young children by promoting different patterns of brain development.' Henderson was referring to a research programme conducted by Professor Laurel Trainor of McMaster University in Hamilton, Ontario, Canada (2006), which established that after a year of musical training children aged between four and six performed better at a standard memory test than did children who were not taught music. In referring to her research Professor Trainor commented: 'This is the first study to show that brain responses in young, musically trained and untrained children change differently over the course of a year. These changes are likely to be related to the cognitive benefit that is seen with musical training.'

The work done at McMaster was notable because, although previous studies had revealed that IQ scores improved for older children taking music lessons, this was the first study to indicate benefits in children so young.

On a cautious note, however, Trainor's sample was only small (12 children) and the programme relied upon the Suzuki method of music teaching, a Japanese approach that encourages children to listen and imitate before they learn to read music, rather than a method more commonly found in the public education system.

These caveats notwithstanding, the McMaster University research has some credibility given that it shows similarity to other work that has shown music tuition to have an influence on thinking skills and brain activity.

Learning and brain activity

In recent years there has been a great deal of work completed examining how brain activity influences learning styles. If we know the type of learner a pupil is, argue the theorists, then we can determine the ideal learning experience for them and maximize their understanding and assimilation of new information. Thus it is that we have a variety of theories to choose from including: 'brain-based learning', which deals with the context of learning; 'communities of practice', which examines the social and interactive nature of learning; 'multiple intelligences', which identifies a variety of 'skills' or 'intelligences' that help us to perceive and understand the world; and 'right and left brain'.

Right- and left-brain theory

This theory of the structure of the brain and the way the mind functions suggests that the right and left hemispheres of the brain control different types of thought processes and that normally each individual has a preference for one type over the other. Experiments have shown that the two hemispheres do in fact influence different activities and it has been possible to categorize them as follows:

Left-brain learners	Right-brain learners
• logical, sequential	• intuitive
• analytical in approach	• holistic in approach
• verbal, respond to direct meaning	• responds to word sound, pitch feeling and emotion
• process information in a linear manner	• processes information in chunks
• objective	• subjective
• punctual	• not always punctual
• pre-plan	• likes to be spontaneous
• prefer formal study approach	• relaxed study environment, music playing

- good memory for names
- likes order, structure and predictable events
- prefers to research/familiarize self ahead of event
- introvert
- ordered, accurate, more formal in approach

- good memory for faces
- happy with surprises, enjoys unpredictability
- wants to learn through direct experience/doing
- extrovert
- visual, tactile, creative, imaginative, demonstrative when talking

Recent research has revealed that in the development of the brain infants begin with right-brain dominance, revealed by a greater blood flow during the first three years of life. By the fourth year the balance has changed and an increased blood flow to the left half of the brain, in the majority of cases, means that the left brain becomes dominant. This left-brain dominance and its associated preferences, referred to above, means that over the years our education system has leaned towards an approach that values most highly the traditional skills of reading, writing and mathematics, thereby favouring the left-brain learner.

The right-brain learner, despite being able to process information very quickly and see connections and relationships, does so in a non-sequential manner and is often seen as disorganized because they do not present information or learning in the traditional, logical format that has come to be seen as the norm. Naturally for teachers this can present a problem, since in most schools they are expected to work within certain conventions and must determine accurately the difference between innovative thinking and slapdash work.

Since we know from studies of stroke victims or patients who have suffered other forms of brain damage that each half of the brain controls the opposite side of the body it would seem logical to assume that we can easily spot left- and right-brain learners. For example, in left-handed people the right side of the brain must be more dominant; therefore they will be the creative ones. Conversely, the right-handed person, controlled by their left brain, will be more logical and analytical. Experience has shown that it is dangerous to generalize. What has been firmly established, however, is the fact that when learning or thinking creatively a person's ability to process information is enhanced when he or she uses both hemispheres of the brain simultaneously and it is in that respect that the study of music is seen to be significant.

Researchers at the University of Montreal (Sergent *et al.* 1992) found that sight-reading musical scores and playing music activated all four lobes of the brain's cortex. Thus we can say that not only does musical activity use both sides of the brain, it does so simultaneously.

While these claims for music are impressive and can be substantiated by research it is important to heed the warning of Dr Alexandra Lamont, researcher and lecturer in Music Psychology at Keele University, Staffordshire. Lamont points out that it is misguided to support any subject or extra-curricular programme solely on the basis of their secondary benefits and it is important to remember that the most important benefit of any music programme is the improvement in pupil's musical development. That being said, Lamont has personally conducted research into participation in musical activities and has concluded that there are definite benefits.

The wider benefits

In the overview section of her paper *The Effects of Participating in Musical Activities* (2003) Lamont discusses recent findings that show that children who take part in musical activities experience higher levels of identification towards their school than children who do not. Three recent studies have revealed that although it is usual to find a gradual decline in pupils' identification with school, as they grow older, this decline is 'halted and even reversed for those children who take part in extra-curricular musical activities' (approximately 40 per cent of all children). Clearly this trend could lead to improved academic achievement and may well influence a child's decision to choose music as an examination option.

While she concedes that extensive research has demonstrated

that music can improve performance by positively affecting IQ, Lamont is keen to point out that the studies that she has conducted relate more to 'the way children feel about themselves, their lessons, and their school in general'. In explaining this she cites the work of Jordan and Nettles (2000) and Mahoney and Cairns (1997), who demonstrated that taking part in extra-curricular activities reduces the risk of school drop out, particularly for those pupils most at risk of doing so. She also makes reference to Degelsmith (2001) who found that children who value school and feel a sense of belonging there go on to achieve higher academic grades.

Summarized findings

Very briefly Lamont found that: 'Having a positive musical identity is linked to ... participating in musical activities, and that this helps children identify with school music lessons and with school itself.'

Implications for those teaching music

Taking part in music was seen by pupils to be a key element in feeling positive about the school music curriculum specifically, and the school in general. In particular pupils were enthused more by playing than by just listening or composing. This enthusiasm for music means that pupils will gain more from the music curriculum up to Year 9 and are more likely to continue it beyond that point. If this is the case, given Lamont's findings the school might reasonably expect that they will see an improvement in performance brought about by increased identification *and* improved IQ.

Benefits for transfer programmes

Having reached her conclusions Lamont goes on to apply them to the problems associated with primary/secondary transfer. She states: 'Since the decline in musical engagement seems to take place on a slower timescale than that of school in general, there may be scope for interventions using music to work with vulnerable children as they move into and through the early years of secondary school.' Furthermore she points out that taking part in music can encourage pupils from socio-economically deprived areas to feel a stronger sense of connection to school itself and this may have secondary benefits for children at risk of social and academic problems in adolescence and beyond. In support of this she cites a recent study by Mahoney and Magnusson (2001). They found that in a project similar to Dadzone (see Chapter 7, page 106), fathers from deprived economic areas who were involved in community activities such as music were more likely to have sons with lower incidence of criminality.

In conclusion then, it seems clear that whatever research one chooses to lay emphasis upon the clear message is that music, through the creative experience it engenders, brings benefit to the individual, socially and intellectually. It is more than just a 'cultural frill' and if it is properly managed and resourced it will bring extensive benefit to the school and the wider curriculum.

5

Music across
the
Curriculum

A brief glance at earlier chapters of this book will reveal that we have already made reference to the cross-curricular relevance of music and how it can enhance attitudes to learning, increase understanding of other subjects, develop transferable skills and deal with whole-school issues such as bullying.

The National Curriculum for England, on its standards site, says:

> One of the three aims of music in the National Curriculum is to develop the skills, attitudes and attributes that can support learning in other subjects and are needed for employment and life. These broader aims are often integral to music education and will be developed as a consequence of quality work in music. The use of music can both enrich learning in other subjects and consolidate musical skills, knowledge and understanding.

Guidance documents for the curriculum in other areas of the UK echo these views and, as in England, make further statements related to flexible learning and inclusion. The new *Curriculum for Excellence* in Scotland, which is currently being introduced and includes expressive arts within its requirements, says: 'The new curriculum will include space for learning beyond subject boundaries, so learners can make connections between different areas of learning. Through cross-curricular activities, young people can develop their organizational skills, creativity, teamwork and the ability to apply their learning in new and challenging contexts.'

A newly launched and revised curriculum for Northern Ireland, which also acknowledges the importance of music, makes reference to what it calls 'connected learning' and says: 'Throughout their school careers, young people need to be motivated to learn and see the relevance and connections in what they are learning. An important part of that process is being able to see how knowledge gained in one subject area can connect to another and how similar skills are being developed and reinforced right across the curriculum.' In Wales, a report prepared for the Welsh National Assembly and presented in April 2004 recommends a new curriculum, to start in September 2008, and acknowledges that the existing curriculum has in practice '... placed greater emphasis on knowledge and content at some expense to the development of skills, ... [and] ... failed to motivate a significant minority ... '.

All of the websites relevant to the education systems in the UK carry extensive exemplar material to support curriculum requirements and make reference both to opportunities for cross-curricular learning and successful projects that have taken place.

Areas that benefit from cross-curricular approaches

The QCA standards website for the English National Curriculum provides some excellent information on this area of curriculum planning. While it does not make extensive reference to Key Stage 1 and 2 schemes, much of what is available for Key Stage 3 is equally applicable and those areas that need development are more than adequately covered by the information that is to be found within the National Curriculum *Excellence and Enjoyment* documents.

Information available on both of the sites makes it clear that music can be used in a variety of ways and in conjunction with almost every subject to enhance both music skills and wider learning.

Music and language

Music can be used to develop language and understanding through the creation and exploration of lyrics and through singing. It can extend vocabulary, bring an increased precision to word selection and encourage variety in the choice of words and methods of expression. When researching ideas, reading and dictionary skills are improved and the recording of ideas encourages the use and improvement of writing and organizational skills.

Music and English

Students can be encouraged to take part in a variety of activities that combine these subjects. Exercises based on themes from literature that encourage students to write songs based upon stories or relationships in books that they are studying are often fruitful. Writing a love song that Romeo might sing to Juliet, tribal music for the aboriginal character in *Walkabout* or a song for Harry Potter's Quidditch team might fire the imagination. Alternatively taking existing poems and setting them to music would not only develop music skills but would also deepen students' knowledge and understanding of the text.

Time, place and culture

Because music is central to almost every culture it is usually accessible to students regardless of their background, culture or ethnic origin. Music, like the other creative arts often reflects the historical setting in which it was created. Thus, the 'jazz age' of the early twentieth century reflected the carefree life people were searching for after the horrors of the First World War. By making connections in this way music can be used to give an insight into other societies, times and social orders. The music might be classical, it might be religious or maybe military. Whatever its origin, music can be linked to other studies offering students an extra dimension when they study history, geography, RE, PSHE, art and design, science, English, modern foreign languages, drama and so on.

Music and history

Using period music in dance sessions can give students an insight into the way people moved and the conventions and formality that influenced them in other times. Once established this can be extended to include drama work, and character studies can be developed.

Music and geography

Folk music in particular can be a rich source for this topic. As well as giving an historical account of events the lyrics and music are often social documents referring to the lives and work of people. Topics including farming, the fishing industry, mining, and heavy industry can all be studied by combining music and geography and exploring existing songs or inventing new ones.

Music and modern foreign languages

Reference is made in Chapter 9 to work on bullying at Chorlton High School Community Arts College, Manchester, involving the writing of songs in the French language. Clearly this idea is transferable to any topic and any of the modern foreign languages might be used.

Music and PSHE

Music is an ideal tool for exploring and illustrating abstract emotions. Thus in a variety of subject areas original music can be used to express ideas or, in the case of existing pieces, to illustrate how composers use their skills to highlight the tensions and emotions that are associated with particular issues. This quality makes music an ideal medium to combine with PSHE. Not only can music and lyrics express difficult ideas relating to moral dilemmas, relationships, lifestyles and so on, it is also a medium that can give a voice to students who might not otherwise wish to join discussions.

Music and mathematics

The structure of a musical score and the metre of lyrics are based upon very strict mathematical rules. The patterns, intervals sequences, rhythms, repetitions and climaxes that occur in music can all be explored mathematically and can be used to engage students' interest. Examples of this could include a study of the music of Beethoven, which reveals the influence of numbers. Patterns can be seen in the number of notes in a melody, the number of bars in a section, the numeric interval between important notes of the main theme and even the choice of opus number. Beethoven uses not only small numbers such as 3 and 5, which may occur anyway, but also larger numbers such as 27 and 33.

Music and science

Music in all of its forms has a direct link with science. How sound is made, how it can be altered, transmitted, amplified and stored are all relevant to science. Even the electricity that is so important to modern music can be approached using music as a starting point. The use of signal generators, oscilloscopes lighting sequencers and equipment such as Soundbeam ® (see Chapter 6, pages 85–7) can be used to clearly illustrate the subjects of frequency, pitch and harmonics.

Music and IT

Given the rise in music technology, the relationship between these two areas is more obvious than it was in the past. There is now a large amount of software available for the composing and recording of music and much of it is financially and technologically within the reach of most schools. Given the increase in the number of specialist arts and technology colleges, schools will usually be able to access expertise at minimal cost should they require training. The very nature of IT means that with this type of cross-curricular link it is easy to combine a number of subjects. This is particularly useful when schools are pursuing whole-school theme based projects.

Wider communication and other transferable skills

As well as written communication, the collective nature of music making improves verbal skills and social interaction. Students learn to negotiate, to compromise and to listen. Rehearsal brings about an ethos of evaluation and instils in students the ideas of constructive evaluation and re-drafting.

Research skills and decision making

The research required to produce relevant lyrics or to compose a piece of music relevant to a particular context or of a given style requires a multitude of skills including discussion, library skills, the use of CDs, DVDs, the internet and so on.

In creating any piece of music students have to make decisions about what is appropriate, or fit for purpose, and in doing so learn to understand the effect that they will have on others, begin to understand the feelings of others and develop empathy as they learn how to relate to and communicate with their audience.

Problem solving

In creating and perfecting music, much of the process relies upon problem solving. The kind of decision making and judgement required benefits students immensely and pay dividends in helping students to improve their work in design and technology.

Case studies from successful cross-curricular projects

In October 2002, as part of its arts curriculum development project, the QCA in England carried out three major studies into the arts in schools. The first collected information about arts provision from 11 schools that gained Artsmark Gold in 2000, the second collected information from a random stratified sample of 21 schools and the third brought together evidence of effective arts practice from 11 schools selected from the first two studies. A brief account of some of the case studies is given below. Full details of the research and the full case studies can be found at www.qca.org.uk/artsalive.

Primary case study: Improving communication skills

This large junior school decided to improve Year 5 pupils' communication skills through an arts-based project on the Tudors. The project developed pupils' understanding of life in Tudor times by exploring the arts used by different social groups.

As a result of the project, there was a marked improvement in pupils' willingness to communicate and the quality of their responses and use of language. Teachers found that pupils gained and retained more than twice the amount of historical knowledge than in previous projects taught in more traditional ways.

The project used music, art and design, dance and drama in combination as a means of studying Tudor life and culminated in a performance.

What the school did

The project was started with a visit to a local Tudor home. This visit was 'interrupted' by actors who brought in a trunk of Tudor artefacts and letters and asked the teachers if they had any value. This set the scene for research and the pupils were asked to find and record information relevant to their enquiry on the Tudors.

Back in school, a cross-subject approach was taken in 'history topic afternoons'. The whole class had a history input from their teacher before being split into small groups and rotated between activities such as historical research, art and design, dance, drama and music. The emphasis in arts activities was on studying Tudor art forms, such as what a pavan sounded like and how the rich were portrayed in portraits.

In music, the pupils were set the task of composing a pavan and a galliard in a group of four to six. All the pupils had to take part in the composition and were involved in appraising each other's work. In creating two contrasting pieces, the pupils explored elements of music such as 3/4, 4/4, tempo and form. Some of their pavans were incorporated into the performance at the end of the term.

The pupils had one topic afternoon each week, plus one music lesson of about an hour per week for the whole of the autumn term. In addition, music compositional tasks were completed during topic afternoons. Towards the end of the project, when preparing for the performance, the pupils often worked as a year group.

On the whole, the pattern of staffing for the year group of three classes was the same as for any topic, although a researcher was given the specific task of observing and collecting data for the project.

The researcher's findings

The researcher found that, as a result of the project, there was a significant improvement in both pupils' willingness to communicate and the quality of their communication. Their use of language improved, as did their ability to interact, give opinions and reasoned answers.

By the end of the Tudor project, the pupils had gained and retained more than twice the amount of knowledge and understanding that they had at the end of a previous control topic.

Teacher observations

The standard of work produced by the pupils was as high, or higher, than the school would normally expect. In music, the compositions showed skill in understanding of melody, structure and form. The project generated an extraordinary enthusiasm and sense of personal involvement. There was a significant increase in the number of Year 5 pupils attending after-school homework club to find out more about the Tudors and develop their research skills.

When given a free choice of writing, several pupils chose to set their stories in a historical context showing a sense of time and place. One Latvian pupil, who had only been in the school system for three months, asked his EAL teacher to help him write some sentences about the Tudors to take back to class. The pupils were clearly more willing to speak and listen to their peers and adults, and were also happier to initiate conversations.

Secondary case study: An attitude-changing performance

This mixed comprehensive school wanted to improve the attitudes of a group of disaffected Year 8 students through an arts-based project. The project, which culminated in a performance, involved students exploring the issue of drugs through music and drama in both timetabled lessons and out-of-hours sessions. Students composed their own music using music technology and developed their ideas through drama. The quality of both the composition and the performance was improved through work carried out in PSHE lessons.

Many of the Year 8 students had low self-esteem at the start of the project. Taking part in a public performance boosted their confidence, generated a great sense of excitement and achievement and showed the rest of the school that learning can be worthwhile and enjoyable.

What did the school want to achieve?

The school's main aim was to improve the attitudes to learning of a group of Year 8 students who caused constant low-level disruption in lessons.

Many of the students in the target group had little self belief and the school felt that taking part in an arts performance might raise their self-esteem. By giving them a 'taste of success', the school hoped to improve their self-image and enhance their relationship with staff and peers.

In subject specific terms the school wanted students to:

- be able to perform with confidence
- understand how hip-hop and rap relate to the time and place in which they are created and heard
- create their own songs using chord sequence, hook lines, lyrics and musical software
- understand how theatre can explore important issues (drug abuse)
- create their own compositions and performance.

What the school did

At the start of the project, students were told that they were going to use work from PSHE for music and drama, and that this would develop their understanding across all three areas and enable them to create a performance.

In PSHE students discussed the effects of drug taking and researched the subject so that they could create the performance.

In music lessons the students:

- listened to and evaluated a variety of hip-hop and rap artists' work, and looked at rap in a historical context
- were shown how to create a chord sequence, taking into consideration factors such as how tonality affects mood (major and minor)
- learned the importance of hook lines to maintain interest in a song
- wrote and structured lyrics, using rhyme beyond basic couplets to affect the rhythm dynamics of the whole piece
- used software such as Cubase VST, Hip Hop Ejay and Micrologic AV to give their performance a professional quality
- were 'mentored' by Year 11 DJs and MCs in the use of mixing decks and rapping.

In drama the students were introduced to a variety of dramatic and theatrical techniques to assist them with the creation and performance of the final piece. All of this was introduced in a non-threatening way to support those who were concerned about the performance. From the start students were encouraged to take decisions and were encouraged to set their own criteria for success so that they felt ownership for the project and were clear about their objectives.

All the teachers involved were careful to ensure that the work was relevant to the students, that they were able to work to their strengths and that learning styles were new and varied in order to break negative cycles that had developed within the group. Working groups were carefully selected so that every member had something to offer and the target of the performance was used to maintain a focus for the work.

The project took 14 weeks in total and was directed by three subject specific staff who structured it to minimize disruption to the timetable. For the first 12 weeks all work took place within designated lessons with extra time offered in after-school sessions. At first attendance at these was poor but as the project progressed they became more popular. During the final two weeks of the project some extra rehearsal time was made available so that the students felt secure prior to the performance.

The research

The school collected evidence of the project's impact by interviewing students before and after the project, by comparing attendance records, behaviour records and student performance data. Staff kept a log of the project, and all students were assessed using National Curriculum criteria. Rehearsals and performances were recorded; comparisons were made between participants and other Year 8 students. Key Stage 2 performance was used as a benchmark. Teacher observation played an important part in the assessment.

Teacher observations

Teachers noticed a vast improvement in confidence and students displayed a real sense of achievement. They displayed pride in their work and their performance and the school noticed a real sense of group identity as students learned to work together and support one another. Students' music and drama skills developed significantly and they were surprised at how good they could be and how much they had to offer.

The improvement in self-esteem brought about improvement in subject areas not covered by the performance. None of these improved characteristics were seen in the group that did not take part in the performance.

As a result of the project, other students (especially low achievers across the year groups) showed increased interest and asked if they could learn skills on the mixing decks and associated technology. The impact of this project exceeded all expectations and the school is now committed to providing similar experiences for all students.

6

INCLUSION

According to the QCA (2004): 'The issue of inclusion is central to the development of music education. The big challenge ahead for music education is to really ensure music is for all.'

All pupils are entitled to having their specific needs met within a broad and balanced music curriculum. QCA set out three general principles for teachers to modify programmes of study so that all pupils are appropriately challenged at all Key Stages:

- setting suitable learning challenges
- responding to pupils' diverse learning needs
- overcoming potential barriers to learning and assessment for individuals and groups of pupils.

Teachers in the 2005 QCA focus group believe that 'music and arts in the curriculum lend themselves to inclusive approaches in ways not available to other subjects'. They give two examples:

1) Music can help engage pupils with learning difficulties by allowing them to express themselves.
2) Music can be useful in encouraging involvement and improving self-confidence, for pupils for whom English is a second language.

If pupils are unable to use their voice, assessment normally requiring the use of it should be discounted and pupils encouraged to develop other areas of the programmes of study.

Gifted and talented

Identifying talent in music can sometimes be hard to define in words. Quality is not defined by complexity but rather it 'sounds right ... skills and techniques are used to communicate an intended mood or effect' (www.qca.org.uk). Talented pupils are able to produce good quality results even at simple tasks and musical expression is as important as accuracy in such responses. Pupils can display signs of talent at all attainment levels.

A common misconception is that any child who has achieved

success, perhaps in graded examinations on an instrument, is 'talented'. Many pupils are given the opportunity to take private peripatetic lessons and begin to progress through graded ABRSM examinations. Certainly some pupils who take this route are talented and this is easy to recognize by their progression. Pupils who are equally talented but have not learned to play an instrument can take longer to identify, as can pupils who are talented at composition or improvisation. The DfES say that musical talent can be identified by 'a child's intense motivation or commitment, temperament and through aspects of personality, which ultimately are reflected through individuality in their art'.

Pupils with talent in music will show evidence of particular ability by:

- A strong sense of self and personal identity and emotional fulfilment through music.
- Bringing their own original and imaginative internal musical ideas to their music making and communicating them to a wider audience.
- Having a special form of sensitivity and feeling, and a need to externalize musical ideas in an expressive way, both in their playing and their compositions.
- An ability to demonstrate a higher level of discernment, intuition and response to both their own musical ideas and the ideas of others.
- Demonstrating a concentration in playing and performance that almost seems to exclude others as they become absorbed in their own expressive world but still able to communicate. (Many exceptionally gifted pupils may wish to work alone when given creative tasks in the classroom rather than engage in group-work with others.)
- Showing a passion and a drive when performing, coupled in some cases with a strong identification with a chosen instrument and its sound and qualities.
- Showing the ability to improvise creatively and expressively.
- Showing a particularly high ability in recalling sounds, imitating musical ideas and conveying them accurately,

though not necessarily through singing. (However it should be noted that although aural capacities may be important in identification, they may not necessarily be a reliable indicator of musical ability, just as musical ability tests may not clearly identify all those highly talented individuals.)

− Having a clear idea of what they wish to play and learn, together with developing a sense of direction in creating their own repertoire of musical material or ideas, both in performance interpretation and composition.

A talented pupil may not show the same ability in all areas of music and will benefit from experiencing a wide range of genres and styles. Particular attention may need to be paid to weaker areas to develop their overall musicianship.

Early identification of talented pupils is beneficial to both teacher and pupil. QCA stress the importance of early exposure to a wide variety of music before and during Key Stage 1. This will enable talented pupils to access the same variety of music with ease later on as pupils will already be familiar with the different ways of organizing sound. As pupils get older they find it harder to appreciate unfamiliar types of music.

All pupils need to be accommodated within class lessons, so it is important for the class teacher to be aware of individual talents and areas needing development. Teachers may need to adapt schemes of work to provide differentiated challenges. In performing tasks, a range of parts increasing in difficulty can be offered to pupils or the chance to use both hands in keyboard work for example. Opportunities for improvisation allow pupils to demonstrate creativity and often uncover hidden talent within a class.

Talented pupils can often find working with others frustrating. Teachers can encourage them to put ideas forward in groups and take the lead in group-work. ICT is a useful compositional resource as it allows pupils to layer musical ideas to produce more complex compositions while working alone.

Talented pupils should be encouraged to take peripatetic lessons and they often benefit greatly from one-to-one tuition. Involvement in extra-curricular activities can also encourage talent and it brings together pupils from different age groups. Often pupils who are talented at music are not generally 'gifted' across a range of subjects – some theories suggest that there are different types of intelligence This brings into question the usefulness of predicted levels that many teachers have to work with at KS3 and beyond. These are based on tests taken in maths, English and science at KS2. While a useful indicator of general intelligence, the results give no indication of musical talent. Despite this, teachers often have to justify to parents or even senior staff why an intelligent child is not talented in music or explain how a musically talented child has exceeded their predicted level.

Assessment for gifted and talented pupils is likely to involve the use of higher than average attainment levels for that particular Key Stage. At Key Stage 1 these are levels 3 and 4 (the average is 2); at Key Stage 2 these are levels 5 and 6 (the average is 4); and at Key Stage 3 these are levels 7 and 8 (the average is 5/6). Gifted and talented pupils may not achieve these kinds of levels across all of the four programmes of study (listening and applying knowledge and understanding, performing, composing and appraising).

Learning difficulties

Everyone has an innate ability to respond to music regardless of any learning difficulties. The idea of music being used as a therapy has been around since the writings of Plato and Aristotle. The Music Therapy Charity say that music can be used to assess and treat people with 'sensory, physical and learning disabilities, mental health problems, emotional and behavioural disturbances and neurological problems'.

Music is an inimitable form of communication that can have a profound effect on pupils with learning difficulties. In particular, QCA report that it offers them opportunities to:

- experience a sense of pride and achievement in their own work

- demonstrate their ability in an area not dependent on language skills
- improve listening, concentration and attention skills
- develop imitation skills
- produce sounds and develop expressive language
- practise turn-taking
- choose, discriminate and justify decisions
- experiment and try new ideas where there are no right or wrong answers
- develop coordination and functional fine motor skills
- support the development of movement and mobility
- encourage cooperation, tolerance and a willingness to work with others
- develop self-discipline and self-confidence
- foster community involvement
- be involved in activities that may provide a fulfilling hobby or pastime and promote lifelong learning.

The programmes of study at all Key Stages can be modified to provide pupils with learning difficulties with an appropriate musical education. Teachers may decide to use material designed for younger pupils or simplify schemes of work, for example. The way in which pupils respond to tasks can also be adapted. The QCA additional inclusion information for music states that to overcome any potential barriers to learning in music, some pupils may require:

- Help in managing the written communication aspects of music, such as the use of symbols, by using larger print and colour codes, multisensory reinforcement and a greater emphasis on aural memory skills.
- Encouragement to use their voices expressively and to use different forms of communication, such as gesture to compensate for difficulties when singing and speaking, and when responding to music.
- Opportunities to learn about music through physical contact with an instrument and/or sound source where they are unable to hear sounds clearly or at all.

- Access to adapted instruments or ICT to overcome difficulties with mobility or manipulative skills.

Such requirements may arise if a pupil has a specific educational need, has a disability or is learning English as an additional language.

Teachers should endeavour to integrate the four aspects of the National Curriculum into all topics covered – these areas are listening and applying knowledge and understanding, performing, composing and appraising.

Listening and applying knowledge and understanding

QCA state that this can help pupils to:

- Listen and develop aural memory, through listening, imitation and turn-taking activities.
- Be aware of the different musical elements, and how these can be organized into musical structures.
- Understand how sounds can be made, produced and described in different ways.
- Understand how music is used for particular purposes, by linking specific sounds, songs and music to particular activities, experiences and moods, by listening to music previously heard live and by producing music individually or as a result of group or classwork.

An example task across the Key Stages could be to play a musical 'Simon Says' where the teacher performs a simple rhythm on a percussion instrument and the pupils copy, either as a class or individually. This can increase in either rhythmic difficulty or with the use of musical elements, for example varying tempo or loudness.

Controlling sounds through singing and playing – performing skills

QCA state that this can help pupils to:

- Participate in songs, possibly through the use of ICT; vocalizing; signing actions; humming a phrase of a melody or using an end word or phrase in a chant, rhyme or song; developing vocal techniques and musical expression.
- Play tuned and untuned instruments, possibly through exploring and interacting with sound making or vibrating objects, playing a variety of instruments using a range of techniques to produce different sound qualities and working to increase awareness and control; performing with others, through activities to develop an awareness of self and others in musical activities, anticipating turns; taking turns; working collaboratively with others with an increasing awareness of their role within the group and their audience.

An example task could be to integrate 'Soundbeam®' into a class performance where pupils use movement to control sound production (see pages 85–7).

Creating and developing musical ideas – composing skills

QCA state that this can help pupils to:

- Create sounds spontaneously through: close attention to adults' imitations of pupils' own sounds; being aware that their movements create sounds; experimenting with sounds and sound makers, including the use of ICT, creating a body percussion sequence, improvising; exploring a range of musical elements in a variety of ways.
- Explore, choose and organize sounds and musical ideas through developing an awareness of how sounds can be made by listening, observing and exploring; developing an

understanding of cause and effect and how sounds can be changed and ordered; demonstrating a preference for particular sounds; making choices; using ICT to create, record, change, combine and refine sounds; playing percussion instruments in a group and adding or taking away one instrument or a group of instruments at a time; using graphic scores to sequence music; playing, comparing and contrasting different arrangements; creating a sound picture using instruments or everyday objects; combining aspects of the same and different musical elements to make a simple musical structure; selecting and combining resources within a given musical structure, genre, style or tradition.

ICT can be used to good effect in composition tasks. Software such as 'Compose World Play' for Foundation to Key Stage 2, 'Compose World Create' for Key Stages 1 and 2 or 'Dance Ejay' for Key Stage 3 students allow the creation of impressive sounding compositions through manipulating pre-recorded samples. Students choose the order and layering of blocks without having to play the ideas in on a keyboard.

Responding and reviewing – appraising skills

QCA state that this can help pupils to:

- Explore and express their ideas and feelings about music, and use a musical vocabulary; develop preferences for particular styles of music; develop an awareness of the similarities and differences between different pieces of music and the feelings and moods they create; respond to music linked to art, pictures, photographs, poems and extracts from books; compare and contrast music by different composers on particular themes, compare and contrast different music by the same composer.
- Make improvements to their own and others' work by developing an awareness of the similarities and differences between sounds; by identifying and comparing sounds; by

listening to and recognizing recordings of their own and others' work; by making changes to their work, and by making and justifying choices about instruments, sounds and music.

Example tasks could involve responding physically to music being played, for example moving faster or slower to reflect the music or using facial expressions to reflect the mood conveyed in a piece of music.

QCA give many examples of activities for these four areas in the document *Planning, Teaching and Assessing the Curriculum for Pupils with Learning Difficulties* (www.nc.net.uk). This also includes ideas for teaching music to visually or hearing impaired pupils.

Soundbeam®

Soundbeam® is a device that converts physical movements into sound. It can be used in several areas in the education sector – special needs, mainstream and dance in particular. QCA recommend the use of it in their materials for pupils with learning difficulties. Soundbeam® uses sensors to detect body movement, which triggers digitally produced sound and image. There can be up to four sensors that send out ultrasonic pulses. These are above the frequencies of audible sound. If these pulses, or 'beams' of sound, are interrupted by an obstacle they are reflected back to the sensor, which can determine the distance of the obstacle by the time taken for the echo to reach the sensor. This information can be used to send MIDI information to a sound module or sampler for example. The beams can be divided into up to 128 sections. Each of these sections can activate a different sound or sounds. The beams have a range of up to six metres. In addition to the four sensors, up to eight switches can be used. These can trigger sounds or effects and are useful for group-work or more complicated pieces. The sounds triggered can be anything from single notes or chords to sound effects or even recorded speech.

Other information, such as video clips or lighting for example, can also be triggered through the use of other software. The sensor can be set to act as a virtual keyboard across a large space or even set to the order of notes in an existing melody, which can then be played by moving along the beam in the correct rhythm.

Soundbeam® is widely used in special education and music therapy. The company say that it 'provides a medium through which even profoundly physically disabled or learning impaired individuals can become expressive and communicative using music and sound'. The nature of Soundbeam® means that even tiny movements can control the resource, which opens up possibilities for those with restricted movement. Performers are no longer limited to playing one instrument at a time; they can be in control of a whole orchestra for example.

Drake Music is an organization that creates opportunities for disabled children and adults to compose and perform music. They make use of both specialist and adapted music technology such as Soundbeam®. This allows disabled individuals to perform as equals with non-disabled musicians and performances are of the highest quality. Soundbeam® can be integrated into mainstream lessons in many ways. It can enable pupils with limited instrumental abilities to trigger drum loops or chords, for example. Up to 12 pupils can control sounds at once in group-work. Soundbeam® was originally invented for dancers to combine sounds with movement. Markers can be put on the floor to indicate particular points that cross the beam so that pupils can see where to move at certain points in the performance. With the added possibility of using visual images, the potential for multimedia performances can be explored.

In 2004 a composer called Martin Kiszko explored this potential to great effect and was named composer of the year for education/community music with 'INUA', a piece of music and multimedia devised with a class of secondary school pupils from Worcester.

There is great potential for using Soundbeam® across the curriculum. The company say that: 'Devising multi-input demonstrations of current topics derived from English literature, history, geography, science, art, as well as dance, drama, music and music technology, can suggest very rewarding ways of presenting new ideas in these subjects.' Maths and science could also use Soundbeam® for investigating sound, frequency and switches, for example.

Assessment using P-scales

P-scales became statutory in 2007. They provide a set of eight P-levels that are to be used for special educational needs (SEN) pupils who are working below level 1 of the National Curriculum. The performance descriptors for P1–3 are the same for all subjects. These embrace general types and ranges of performance that SEN pupils may show.

Pupils working at levels P1 to P3 should:

- P1 (i): Encounter activities and experiences. May be passive or resistant. May show simple reflex responses. Any participation is fully prompted.

 P1 (ii): Show emerging awareness of activities and experiences. May have periods when they appear alert and ready to focus their attention on certain people, events, objects or parts of objects. May give intermittent reactions.
- P2 (i): Begin to respond consistently to familiar people, events and objects. React to new activities and experiences. Begin to show interest in people, events and objects. Accept and engage in co-active exploration.

 P2 (ii): Begin to be proactive in their interactions. Communicate consistent preferences and affective responses. Recognize familiar people, events and objects. Perform actions, often by trial and improvement, and remember learned responses over short periods of time. Cooperate with shared exploration and supported participation.
- P3 (i): Begin to communicate intentionally. Seek attention through eye contact, gesture or action. Request events or activities. Participate in shared activities with less support. Sustain concentration for short periods. Explore materials in increasingly complex ways. Observe the results of their own

actions with interest. Remember learned responses over more extended periods.

P3 (ii): Use emerging conventional communication. Greet known people and may initiate interactions and activities. Remember learned responses over increasing periods of time and may anticipate known events. May respond to options and choices with actions or gestures. Actively explore objects and events for more extended periods. Apply potential solutions systematically to problems.

Levels P4–8 can be used if pupils begin to show skills, knowledge and understanding in music:

- P4: Pupils use single words, gestures, signs, objects, pictures or symbols to communicate about familiar musical activities or name familiar instruments. With some support, they listen and attend to familiar musical activities and follow and join in familiar routines. They are aware of cause and effect in familiar events. They begin to look for an instrument or noisemaker played out of sight. They repeat, copy and imitate actions, sounds or words in songs and musical performances.
- P5: Pupils take part in simple musical performances. They respond to signs given by a musical conductor. They pick out a specific musical instrument when asked. They play loudly, quietly, quickly and slowly in imitation. They play an instrument when prompted by a cue card. They listen to, and imitate, distinctive sounds played on a particular instrument. They listen to a familiar instrument played behind a screen and match the sound to the correct instrument on a table.
- P6: Pupils respond to other pupils in music sessions. They join in and take turns in songs and play instruments with others. They begin to play, sing and move expressively in response to the music or the meaning of words in a song. They explore the range of effects that can be made by an instrument or sound maker. They copy simple rhythms and musical patterns or phrases. They can play groups of sounds indicated by a simple picture or symbol-based score. They begin to categorize percussion instruments by how they can be played.

- P7: Pupils listen to music and can describe music in simple terms. They respond to prompts to play faster, slower, louder, softer. They follow simple graphic scores with symbols or pictures and play simple patterns or sequences of music. Pupils listen and contribute to sound stories, are involved in simple improvisation and make basic choices about the sound and instruments used. They make simple compositions.
- P8: Pupils listen carefully to music. They understand and respond to words, symbols and signs that relate to tempo, dynamics and pitch. They create their own simple compositions, carefully selecting sounds. They create simple graphic scores using pictures or symbols. They use a growing musical vocabulary of words, signs or symbols to describe what they play and hear. They make and communicate choices when performing, playing, composing, listening and appraising.

QCA exemplify subject specific levels 1–8 in the document *Planning, Teaching and Assessing the Curriculum for Pupils with Learning Difficulties* (www.qca.org.uk).

Overseas arrivals

As language is not a pre-requisite for musical communication, music can often be an effective subject for new arrivals to be integrated into. QCA (www.qca.org.uk) comment that: 'Creative approaches that are accessible to all pupils including those learning EAL can assist teachers in including new arrivals fully.' Again, teachers are able to adapt programmes of study to suit the needs of individual pupils where appropriate. QCA (www.qca.org.uk) also note: 'An awareness of pupils' language skills and cultural knowledge can help teachers provide activities that are relevant and accessible.'

Wherever possible teachers should use pupils' previous experiences to build upon in the music curriculum.

Respect for all

The Race Relations Act from 2000 requires all schools to promote racial equality. For many pupils, music embodies the culture in which they live. Learning about music from different cultures is a unique way of teaching pupils to value diversity. The National Curriculum's programmes of study and the QCA's Schemes of Work promote opportunities to value diversity and challenge racism. Music from different times and cultures features in the exemplar schemes of work for all Key Stages.

QCA devised three key areas of knowledge and understanding that need to be covered to enable pupils to appreciate all music:

1. understanding how music is constructed
2. understanding how music is produced
3. understanding how music is influenced by its context.

The third of these areas has the most influence in valuing diversity. Once pupils can see the role of music within the surroundings of a particular time and culture, the often unfamiliar methods of construction and production have more relevance. QCA comment in the 2004/5 music report that: 'The different cultural backgrounds of learners and their parents can be used to enhance a school's curriculum and can inform and contribute to musical activities.' Teachers should make use of resources in the surrounding locality and use live performances to introduce unfamiliar styles of music wherever possible.

QCA (www.qca.org.uk) report that teaching music from different cultures can help pupils to understand and appreciate:

- **Cultural difference**
  There is a wide range of different kinds of music, and this diversity is caused by the cultural context that affects how and why music is created, performed and received.
- **Cultural identity**
  It is shared values, interests, experiences and codes of behaviour that give us a sense of belonging and identity,

and these influences are reflected in the types of music we choose to listen to and enjoy.

- **Cultural complexity**
  People in Britain live in a variety of different cultural contexts and can have different cultural identities, for example the family, friends, the school, the region, the country and the world. Music can reflect different identities and demonstrate cultural interaction and fusion.
- **Cultural change**
  All of us contribute to the cultural contexts in which we live, and each individual can change these contexts for good or ill.

Extra-curricular inclusion

Extra-curricular activities and performance opportunities should also allow for inclusion and not just be a showcase for the elite or the 'classical' musicians. Schools should have a variety of groups that cater for different abilities and reflect a range of styles of music. Some schools have activities such as karaoke club. Beginner groups are a good way of showcasing progress made in extra-curricular lessons and can give pupils performing opportunities to aim for. Advanced groups give other pupils something to aspire to and provide appropriate challenges to members.

Parental encouragement plays a big part in determining whether or not children continue to play a musical instrument. The *Young People Music and Participation Project* completed in 2001 by Keele University reported that: 'Children who stay involved in learning to play an instrument believe that their parents are supportive of this activity far more than children who give up.' Regular feedback in the form of concerts is likely to promote such support and encouragement from parents, who often contribute financially to peripatetic lessons.

7

MUSIC ACROSS
THE WHOLE
SCHOOL

Before any school can count itself successful it must be confident in the assertion that all its pupils feel safe in the school environment, feel valued, value others and enjoy the learning experience. Unless a school is able to feel confident about these aspects of school life it cannot claim to be fully educating its pupils and it cannot expect them to achieve their full potential.

Although there are some differences in detail and the wording of curriculum legislation may differ slightly, schools in all of the constituent countries of the UK are required in broad terms to provide their pupils with the same basic educational experiences. Paraphrased, these are:

- providing opportunities for all pupils to learn and achieve
- safeguarding and promoting social, moral, spiritual, mental and physical aspects of life, learning and well-being
- preparing pupils adequately for the challenges and responsibilities of adult life in the wider world.

Throughout the UK the legislation recognizes that there is no single right way to deliver the timetable and discharge these responsibilities. What is clear, however, is that the delivery of particular subjects is central to the philosophy of a National Curriculum and the logical step from that is, as well as the body of knowledge attached to each of those subjects, there should be scope and provision for the teaching of the wider aspects of the curriculum that are required as part of these responsibilities. While this might not be entirely possible in every subject it undoubtedly will be across the curriculum as a whole, and in the case of music the opportunities will be numerous and varied.

Music and behaviour

Although some parades of shops and railway stations in England have adopted the practice, playing classical music to annoy/drive away unruly groups of young people is not quite the behaviour management solution that most schools are looking for! However, schools are increasingly looking towards the use of background music to establish an atmosphere. The 'Big Writing' programme is just one initiative that suggests the playing of music to create an atmosphere and encourage students in their extended writing.

Many schools already have music playing in their public areas and Gwyn Lloyd-Jones, headteacher of Ysgol-y-Ddol in Rhydymwyn North Wales speaks enthusiastically about its introduction and use in his school. While some would disparagingly call it wallpaper, Gwyn is in no doubt that music played in the entrance area of the school sends out an unambiguous message to pupils and parents making it clear that the expected atmosphere in the school is one of calm. Not only, says Gwyn, does this have a positive effect on pupils, particularly those sent there for disciplinary reasons, it also sends out an unequivocal message to visitors to the school and Gwyn is convinced that in some cases it has reduced the likelihood of confrontation when some parents have visited the school. Gwyn states: 'The effect of this is to promote cooperation and to discourage the view that teachers are on a different side to parents and pupils.'

Structuring a music lesson

The structure of music lessons can vary greatly depending on factors such as the age and ability of the pupils and the topics to be covered.

It is useful to have the classroom set out in the best way before the lesson begins. Group-work may be more productive with tables pushed together, for example. Delegate this task to some pupils before the other pupils enter the classroom. Make sure that resources are ready and keep on top of instrumental repairs. Checking adaptors and so on can be a useful task for any detained pupils to carry out. Damaged instruments convey the impression that they are not valued and this can have a negative influence on attitudes.

In general, lessons can be divided into three sections – start, main part and summary. Singing can be a great way to grab the pupils' attention and can begin as soon as the pupils enter the classroom. There are several companies, such as Ameritz (www.ameritz.co.uk), who produce good quality backing tracks to popular songs. Karaoke backing CDs are also useful to have in the classroom. The start of the lesson should include the aims and place it in context of the scheme of work and the previous lesson. Formal procedures, such as dealing with homework and registration, will usually occur in this section.

The main section of the lesson should be the longest period and should aim to cater for different learning styles such as visual, aesthetic and kinaesthetic. Lessons should ideally integrate the three strands of the curriculum – listening, performing and composing. Try to break up the main section of the lesson so that the class is brought back together. Any common problems can be dealt with and tasks will work better if broken into manageable chunks. The prospect of having to perform their work in front of the class is generally a good motivational factor when leaving groups alone to work. Use a variety of individual, pair and group-work across the schemes of work. When listening to long sections of music give the pupils a focus. For example: How does the music make you feel? Which instrument plays the tune? When following scores, try stopping the recording every so often to ask 'What bar are we up to in the score?' This helps to sustain concentration. The pupils should remain as active as possible in the lesson.

The lesson summary is a chance to consolidate learning and relate it to the following lesson. Pupils might be given a short written task such as a missing gaps exercise or a rehearsal diary to fill in if the task is to continue next time. Homework can be set in this part – this could be learning lyrics, research or preparing a presentation for example. Homework should not just be given for the sake of it. Make it as relevant to the current task and as varied as possible.

Classroom management for music

Music, by the very nature of the subject, is concerned with the production of sound. When handled well, music lessons can be productive and enjoyable for everyone. If handled badly, lessons can be a cacophonic disaster! Great consideration needs to be given to the conduct of practical tasks in particular. The first few lessons with a new class are vital in establishing rules and routines that are used consistently, ideally across the department if there is more than one music teacher.

Using instruments

It can be helpful to select instrument monitors to give out instruments and so on, while the teacher supervises the process looking out for potential problems. Monitors can change weekly or every term and be rewarded for their help.

The first, and most natural, reaction when handed a musical instrument is to play it.

This is not always an appropriate response when handling a class of 30 eager pupils with a percussion instrument!

When using xylophones, the temptation to play them can be lessened by handing out the beaters last. When using keyboards, the power can be left off until the task is ready to begin. Explain the reason for the rules to your class and decide upon the consequence for misuse of an instrument. Some teachers allow time for a 'bash' of an instrument at the beginning of a lesson for a controlled length of time. It can also be effective to allow some free time at the end of a lesson as a reward for good behaviour. Zero tolerance is often the best way to deal with the dreaded 'demo button' pressing on keyboards; that is the keyboard is confiscated and a written task given.

Pupils should also be taught to respect each other by not talking or touching instruments when listening to performances within the class. Although lessons can feel like a military operation initially, good habits will endure and lessons become much easier in subsequent years with the same pupils.

Using computers

Interactive whiteboards or digital projectors are an invaluable resource for demonstrating computer-based tasks to a whole class. Involving pupils in the demonstration also helps to sustain concentration.

An extremely useful resource for managing computer-based lessons is 'Classnet' (see www.keyzone.com/classnet). The teacher can project their own screen to individual pupil monitors or the whole classes' for demonstrating tasks. Any screen in the room can be accessed by the teacher, who can communicate with pupils (individual or all) through headphones with the use of a microphone. The teacher can darken the pupils' screens to gain their attention and pupils can listen to each other's work if the teacher projects it onto their screens.

Posters displaying basic functions are useful to have around the classroom, as is a reminder of how to leave the computer at the end of the lesson, for example headphones on monitor, computer logged off.

As with any practical task, it is useful to bring the class back together at intervals during the lesson to hear where individuals are up to or to discuss any common problems the pupils are encountering.

Noise

Make friends with your neighbours – communicate with fellow teachers who teach within earshot of your classroom. Let them know when noisy situations are unavoidable, in practical assessments for example and be creative with 'quieter' lessons planned to avoid the disruption of examinations in other subjects.

Choice of music

Aim to use as wide a range of music as possible from across the world and across the centuries. Using up-to-date material is a guaranteed way of grabbing attention and pupils will be more open minded about other genres if they can understand how their own music has developed from previous styles. Ask the pupils to bring in music of their choice and use it wherever you can, for example use a reoccurring song riff as a way to introduce the technique of an ostinato and then perhaps follow with a lesson on ground bass in Baroque music.

Sample lesson plan

Class – Year 7
Topic – the orchestra
Duration – one hour

Aims/objectives:

By the end of the lesson all students will be able to:

- remember the four families in the orchestra – a recap of previous knowledge
- understand that each family is made up of different pitched instruments
- aurally identify the four families and instruments within each.
- begin to learn the first section of *Harry Potter* on keyboard.

By the end of the lesson some students will be able to:

- pick out specific instruments within a large arrangement.

Extension task:

- learn a longer section of the music.

Resources:

- *Harry Potter* CD
- CD recordings demonstrating specific instruments in each family

- CD recordings demonstrating instrumental families
- *Harry Potter* score and CD backing from www.musicroom.com
- orchestra layout diagram
- instrument pictures for students to hold up
- keyboards and adaptors
- homework sheet.

Introduction:

- Play excerpts from *Harry Potter* as students enter room.
- Settle and register.
- Play excerpts again with questions and answers. For example: Which instrument do you think is playing the melody? Increase difficulty level of questions.
- Share aims of lesson.

Main part:

- Recap names of orchestral families – write on board. Give examples of large and small instruments from each family. Play short examples of music (various pieces) demonstrating each instrument, for example piccolo and then bassoon, trumpet and then tuba and so on.
- Display the layout of the orchestra and divide the class into similar sections. Hand out large pictures of instruments to each student, for example violins, violas, cellos, basses.
- Play excerpts featuring individual sections – students to hold pictures up when they hear their section.
- Introduce practical task – students to learn the first part of the *Harry Potter* theme on keyboard. Hand out scores and demonstrate along to backing track. Clap rhythms of first part of melody. Comment on chromatic melody – write in vocabulary list in rehearsal diaries.
- Monitors to hand out keyboards then adaptors. Time limit given. Students practice, teacher circulates to help.
- Individual students to play where up to so far – more advanced students to learn next section. If time allows, more rehearsals to follow.

- Next lesson, class to rehearse again and perform to backing track. This can be individually assessed.
- Monitors put keyboards away while other students fill in rehearsal diaries – monitors to do this at home.

Summary:

- Recap aims and questions to test orchestral knowledge.
- Hand out homework sheet – fill in blanks.

Research and case studies

Writing in the *British Journal of Special Education* (Volume 25, No. 2) in June 1998, Dr Susan Hallam and John Price of the University of London Institute of Education reported the findings of their research into the effect of music on learning. Using carefully controlled research methods Hallam and Price worked at a school educating pupils with emotional and behavioural difficulties. They chose ten pupils who displayed a high frequency of disruptive behaviour. The pupils, while learning mathematics, were played (or not played as the experiment demanded) 'calming music'. The pupil's perception of the music was ascertained before the commencement of the experiment. In all cases the researchers observed, 'a marked improvement in behaviour and mathematical performance'. In reporting their findings Hallam and Price acknowledged that there were variations in improvement depending upon the type of emotional and behavioural disturbance but cited other work in the field in their abstract and concluded that the positive effect of music had been demonstrated by their work.

Once teachers accept that music can enhance learning rather than be a distraction in the classroom then they can begin to see the benefits that might be derived. We are already a long way from the Victorian notion that silence in a classroom is the only effective learning environment. If we develop our thinking further and employ some of the findings above then the potential to enhance learning will be released. Teachers who have used music in the classroom (including Malcolm P, an art teacher from the north-west of England) have discovered how wide the benefits can be. As well as the calming influence and consequent improvement in behaviour brought about by the music, Malcolm also discovered that his pupils identified more with his subject, felt more ownership of the teaching space and were more open to cooperation. This cooperation was practised when the pupils chose the music. The ability to compromise and make decisions was enhanced when pupils were required to select genre and appropriate volume. Additionally, because the pupils saw the music as a positive enhancement of their learning environment, it became a useful bargaining tool when agreeing codes of practice for the classroom.

Further evidence of the positive effects of music is contained in the QCA 'Arts Alive' website at www.qca.org.uk/artsalive. Included in this section is information on the use of music to improve social skills and behaviour in schools. Since some of the case studies are also cross curricula, a more detailed examination of the work has been included in Chapter 7.

Music self-esteem and achievement

All teachers know that students learn differently and recent approaches to education in the UK have advocated that a greater emphasis be placed on students' preferred learning styles during the planning and delivery of lessons. There is no doubt that some students can become passionate about music and that some believe it is the only area in which they can succeed. Such students derive a vast amount of self-esteem from music. They are able to achieve, they are often able to perform in front of parents and peers and their ability is something that other students admire and respect.

In our own experience and through work we have carried out on the subject, we have seen students, who might otherwise have been the target of bullying, grow in confidence and form stronger relationships as a result of their involvement in music. In other cases (for example, see the report on Chorlton High

101

School, pages 116–19) students' success in music has led them to develop an interest in other areas of the curriculum, thereby continuing to attend school and achieving more than might have been predicted. The effects of non-completion of statutory education and its association with future criminal and or aberrant behaviour are widely documented and more information can be found in the Continuum publication *Getting the Buggers to Turn Up* (2005).

These specific successes notwithstanding, music can claim to produce the same beneficial effects in all students, improving thinking skills, decision-making, social skills and confidence, thereby producing an overall improvement in performance.

The listening programme

This system is an aural stimulation programme that has been used in some schools to enhance the performance of students and improve their behaviour. The main purpose of the programme is to improve listening skills by stimulating the muscles in the inner ear. The system consists of eight CDs containing largely classical music, which has been re-mastered to emphasize certain frequencies. The knowledge that the right hemisphere of the brain is responsible for motor skills and information processing is central to the success of this method. Sounds received by the left ear, the input mechanism for the right hemisphere of the brain, are designed to exploit that dominance and teachers using the system have noted improvements in behaviour and performance including:

- improved language skills – speaking and listening
- improved sequential processing
- improved coordination
- improvements in reading, writing, spelling and memory capabilities
- increased attention span
- improved motor skills and confidence.

All of the above have brought about improved behaviour and achievement.

Primary/secondary transfer

Research by Homerton College Cambridge and the National Foundation for Education Research (NFER) found that 40 per cent of students lose motivation and make no progress in the year after transfer. This figure was substantially the same throughout the UK. While the problems associated with transfer are complex, and this book would not pretend that it can offer a comprehensive solution, it is nevertheless true that the use of music has proved effective in some schools.

Bridgewater Specialist Performing Arts College in Warrington have been conducting an extensive transfer programme for several years. Director of the Arts College, Gerrie Shadwell, points out that while the programme involves an input from all of the arts the contribution of music is significant and real benefits to the progress of students and links with parents have been seen. The important factor in the transfer programme is the fact that it is not restricted to the summer term or early September but carries on throughout the year. All the arts staff at the school have community time and visit the feeder primaries on a regular basis, organizing arts sessions that include playing, composing and singing. Pupils have the opportunity to perform in a choir that spans the Key Stages and thus meet with older students before they join the school. The work of the choir and pieces created in the arts sessions are frequently performed at the school, giving pupils a chance to become familiar with the staff and the buildings and allowing their parents to form a link with the school.

As well as creating small-scale pieces, Bridgewater has commissioned original works for joint performance by primary and secondary students. One such piece, a cantata about the building of the Bridgewater canal, gave rise to the school's first major transfer programme. Since then their work has developed in scale with teachers spending time in the primary schools creating and composing pieces with Year 6 pupils. This forms the centrepiece of a six-week arts project at the start of Year 7 and culminates in a major performance involving all of the new students. Gerrie has no doubt the project will grow and that it may well, given its success, be adapted for use across the authority. She speaks enthusiastically about the positive outcomes that include self-esteem, self-discipline, a sense of belonging and a motivation to learn. With the school's relatively recent award of second specialism in maths and science she is certain that the transfer programme, with music and the arts at its centre, will become even more cross curricula.

Music and EAL pupils

According to the QCA website: 'Music is a subject into which many newly arrived children can easily be integrated. Most children can express themselves creatively through music and children can learn to express themselves non-verbally through it. This can boost the self-esteem of newly arrived children because they can participate fully in lessons even though their English language may still be limited.' It is widely accepted that music is an excellent tool for inclusion and more detailed information can be found in Chapter 6.

The needs of pupils for whom English is an additional language (usually referred to as EAL pupils) are referred to on the DfES standards site and on the QCA website. While it would be pointless to duplicate all of that information here there are nevertheless some central points that teachers should be aware of.

One of the strengths of music is that most pupils will respond to it in some way. The majority can learn to express themselves non-verbally through it and are therefore able to participate in lessons even though they have a limited ability in the target language. This participation not only raises the self-esteem of EAL pupils but also, because of the collaborative nature of music making, gives them an ideal opportunity to be immersed in the target language and to quickly improve their vocabulary.

However, having said all of that, teachers must remember:

- Not all pupils have prior experience of music.
- Music may have a specific meaning for them.
- Some cultures embrace a musical tradition while in others it is unacceptable.
- Music may be seen as low status or be discouraged for religious reasons.
- Not every culture uses the same musical notation. Pupils may need to become acquainted with the new form.

Despite these caveats the real bonus that teachers will be able to exploit when using music to include EAL pupils is the opportunity to enrich the lives of the whole student cohort. Apart from the raising of an EAL pupil's self-esteem the other key fact with music is its accessibility for all pupils. The fact that pupils can explore a variety of musical styles together, and that the indigenous pupils can relate to the role of music in a culture and see the connections it makes at all levels, will undoubtedly enhance understanding and speed up the process of inclusion.

Connecting with parents

Involving parents in the education of their children has been shown to bring benefits to all aspects of the process. The problem facing some schools is how to draw the parents in and involve them in the first place. Though by no means a panacea, music is often a useful starting point. It is something that pupils take home by recounting their enjoyment of a particular activity or by singing a song that has brought them particular enjoyment. It is something that parents enjoy, often recalling pleasant moments from their own school years, when they get an opportunity to see their children perform. The importance of concerts and performances cannot be overstated and more details about their organization can be found in Chapter 11.

Involving dads

The work of the YMCA through their 'Dads and Lads' programme has shown how sharing activities can positively influence self-esteem, social skills and educational achievement. The 'Dadzone' in South Cumbria has followed this lead and has used music as a key element. A community-based band of dads who perform songs about fatherhood and childhood and enjoy sharing songs with children, 'Dadzone' has organized and supported community events in the region. It has produced 'song boxes', which contain books, musical instruments and props based around a nursery rhyme theme. These are lent out to families through a toy library in Barrow Island, a Sure Start area, with the aim of encouraging the sharing of music and books in homes. A Millennium Award enabled the group to produce a double CD of original music, poetry and song. The dads wrote and recorded these songs through regular meetings, in which they worked together and reflected on their experiences of growing up in the area. This gave them the opportunity to express and discuss their feelings about family relationships, in a supportive environment, and was the first time that some of the dads had written for pleasure since their school days. The dads found that it was quite tricky to pitch the language of the songs at the right level and make them simple and repetitive enough for children and parents to follow and have fun adding their own lyrics. They feel that they succeeded and hope that the project will help children to develop new language, rhyming skills and even writing for a purpose.

8
APPRECIATING THE ART FORM

Listening

Hearing is developed in the womb at approximately 20 weeks after conception. A study by Lamont (2001) demonstrated how babies can remember and show preference for music that they were played up to three months before being born.

Listening to music is the one aspect of music that probably everyone, without exception, does. It accompanies many people's daily activities, whether it is listening to the radio playing in the car or a CD selected to create a particular ambience at home.

Ever since the popularity of rock 'n' roll in the 1950s, listening to music has become firmly rooted in youth culture. On average, teenagers listen to music for approximately 2½ hours a day. Listening to music and observing artists can influence everything from friendship groups to fashion and helps to create a sense of identity. The Omnibus Survey by Youth Music in 2006 reported that 91 per cent of 7–19 year olds confirmed that they liked listening to music.

Young children tend to hear a considerable amount of music during the day. Lamont reports for the BBC website that: 'Most of the time the children are hearing music in recorded format, from the television, children's websites (CBeebies is a popular choice), CDs and tapes, and the radio.' Pop music is the most frequently played type of music that children encounter, mainly due to the musical tastes of parents and older siblings. In 1993, 'The Mozart Effect' was born at the University of California. Students were found to have increased spatial-temporal reasoning after listening to ten minutes of Mozart's Sonata for Two Pianos in D Major. These findings have been exploited by many companies who have used classical music to help sell baby brain-boosting products. Further research since 1993, such as studies by Dr Rauscher, has shown that many types of music can have a beneficial effect on spatial-temporal thinking. Children who learn to play the piano show increased skills in this area. Lamont comments: 'The keyboard seems to be most effective because it's a spatial layout, and music itself is arranged over time, so you have both elements that will help develop spatial-temporal thinking.'

Young children tend to like all styles of music but often prefer fast music to slow.

Experiencing live performances

Hearing a live orchestra for the first time is a memorable and often overwhelming experience. As part of the music manifesto, the government has pledged to give every pupil in the UK access to hearing a live orchestral performance.

Naomi Elliott-Newman is the coordinator for the north-west pathfinder. She described the big impact that performance projects have had on pupils when the Hallé Orchestra has gone into schools to perform. Seventy per cent of the orchestra players choose to involve themselves in educational outreach projects because of the enjoyment and opportunities they provide to pupils.

Performing

Pre-school music groups have become increasingly popular among parents of young children. Groups such as 'Rhythm Time' and 'Monkey Music' run classes across the country for the under fives. Rhythm Time say: 'We instil a love and under-standing of music from an early age, while at the same time developing confidence, creativity, imagination, listening and coordination ... the children learn at a very early age that making music with others is a wonderful, exciting experience. Something they will never forget.'

The Omnibus Survey revealed that 39 per cent of 7–19 year olds are engaged in some form of active music making. Initiatives such as 'Wider Opportunities' (see page 32) are making progress in increasing the uptake of primary school pupils involved in learning to play an instrument; many of these pupils also become involved in group performing.

What's the point if you're not musical?

The majority of pupils who take part in active music making do not go on to become professional musicians or even end up working in a music-related career. So what is the point in taking part in musical activities?

Ronald Frost is the Director of Music at St Ann's Church, Manchester. He held several senior positions at the Royal Northern College of Music for the main part of his career. Much of his time has been spent directing church choirs. He believes that there are numerous benefits to being part of a musical group, and says ' . . . teamwork, friendship, musical instruction, and a lifetime love of music. It is character building and instils discipline – punctuality for example. It is beneficial to health for a variety of reasons.'

Research commissioned by QCA in the 2003/4 report shows that all pupils 'believe that they can be good at some parts of music, even if they think they are not good at the subject'. This research challenges all notions of music education being primarily for those who have a musical talent.

Naomi Elliott-Newman commented that feedback from teachers concerning the benefits to pupils involved in pathfinder performance projects is always positive. They comment on increased confidence and the improvements in pupils' attention span. Often the benefits are only realized after the project and are generally not the reason for involvement initially. Kath, a student who was involved in extra-curricular music at secondary school commented: 'I made friends with people I wouldn't normally have come across . . . I found choir fun and relaxing.' Rachel, now a solicitor, commented: 'I used to love performing in concerts and the sense of achievement I felt when performing in front of my family.'

Theory

The importance of music theory should also be considered. The ABRSM require candidates to demonstrate musical literacy with a pass in Grade 5 theory, Grade 5 practical musicianship or Grade 5 jazz in order to progress to practical examinations at Grades 6, 7 and 8. They state: 'As instrumental skills progress, development in music theory and musicianship becomes increasingly important in helping students to perform with sensitivity, understanding and confidence.' Ronald Frost firmly believes in the importance of musical literacy and has concerns at the way music education has progressed at top levels. He now earns a living from accompanying and training choirs and giving organ recitals. He has been able to have several career options within the field of music because he had thorough training as a student. Ronald believes that we are now producing a generation of people who are musically illiterate. He thinks that music scholars should be able to sight read and have good aural training.

Indeed, in the QCA review of standards at GCSE and A level (2007) some of the comments concerning A level music provision include: 'It was judged that the level of aural perception skills had fallen ... In some cases, candidates were able to bypass aspects such as musical techniques and literacy.'

Composition

Composition is the area that causes most apprehension in teachers and pupils. On entering formal education, most children have listened to different types of music – usually without especially thinking about it (for example, music on the television or music played in the car). Most children have performed music – usually through singing with parents or in pre-school groups. Not many children have attempted composing or creating their own music. Non-specialist teachers tend to find this area the hardest to cover and even secondary music teachers can find it daunting if they are not confident in their own compositional abilities.

Composition at a higher level can be a complex process that amalgamates many aspects of musical knowledge, skills and understanding. This is no different to performing at a high level and therefore should not deter anyone from embarking on the

111

process. Composition is simply the art of organizing sounds over time. Patterns are often used and these can range from simple to more complex. There are no right or wrong answers when attempting to compose. Some attempts will work better than others, and with exposure to other pieces of music ideas will develop. Pupils may begin with copying elements from existing pieces. In time they will develop their own musical vocabulary and enough confidence to experiment.

In school concerts, the aim is often that the music will sound good. Pieces are rehearsed for weeks in preparation and a perfect performance is the goal. Not many concerts feature original compositions by students before GCSE level, where composing is a compulsory area of assessment. It is extremely rewarding for students and parents to hear their own original compositions performed in a concert. Teachers who promote such activities will see students flourish as they progress and become more confident composers. Some schools organize carol-writing competitions where the music teachers create an accompaniment to go with the students' ideas. One student who had their pieces performed in such events commented: 'I was really proud to hear everyone singing my song – I'll never forget it!'

Sarah, an experienced composer, explains how she began composing: 'I got a keyboard for Christmas which had automated backings – you just had to press one key at a time to generate a preset accompaniment with chords, bass and drums. I began to experiment with writing tunes over the top and developed from there.'

Pupils can be encouraged to experiment with simple percussion instruments at home or school. Technology is often a good way to encourage pupils to compose. Relatively cheap keyboards allow pupils to generate accompaniments with one key and, as in Sarah's case, this can lead them to experiment with their own ideas. Computer software such as 'Compose World 2' lets younger pupils 'compose' by ordering and layering pre-recorded blocks. 'Dance Ejay' is similar, but more suitable for older students.

9

EXAMPLES OF GOOD PRACTICE

Choosing the examples

During our research when writing this book, it was abundantly clear that examples of good practice abound in schools everywhere and on that basis it is impossible to single out any and declare them to be the archetype that all should turn to for inspiration and guidance. On that basis we have chosen to include examples based on the work of an English secondary school, a local education authority, a primary school and a specialist teacher of singing. While their work is not necessarily unique it is nevertheless diverse and effective and, since it is carried out on a daily basis in ordinary schools, it is work that could be readily adapted by teachers everywhere should they be so minded. As well as reporting the work we also felt it was important to review it and this is done briefly at the end of the chapter.

Chorlton High School Community Arts College, Manchester

Chorlton High School is an economically and ethnically mixed intake school about three miles from the centre of Manchester. It is immediately adjacent to a borough, (which has retained selection), within ten minutes drive of two private grammar schools (which have a national reputation), and an even shorter distance from a leading private school that has recently gained City Academy Status.

Zoë Morris, deputy head of the school and Director of Arts College provision, explained that given the range of opportunity in the area Chorlton High has set out to provide a distinctive curriculum that is at once diverse, inclusive and enriching for all students regardless of age background or ability.

The school is a 12 form 11–18 comprehensive with an average of 300 students in each year group. All students do an arts GCSE. Indeed it is possible for them to do four arts subjects at examination level, but most are encouraged to take a broader curriculum and given the opportunity to extend their arts involvement through an extensive range of 'out of school' activities. By Year 10, 50 per cent of students take music as an examination option.

Zoë is keen to point out that the foundations for involvement in music are laid at primary school level. Chorlton has six main partner primaries and primary trained staff, employed by the school, work in every school for at least one half-day session per week throughout the year. Often this work is translated into performances that are staged both in the primary school and in the arts college theatre and usually involve collaboration between primary and high school pupils.

In this way the arts quickly become central to students' concepts of learning and the question of primary/secondary transfer is significantly addressed.

Music makers

This scheme was developed to address the needs of those students who find difficulty engaging with school and relating to its values by giving them the opportunity to work alongside musicians. The musicians are *not* teachers. They live in the 'real' world and their brief is to work with the students and help them to achieve and realize self-esteem and purpose through music. The intention and almost invariable outcome is that a student's involvement in music very quickly leads to their involvement in other areas of the curriculum. The purpose of learning is seen because it helps them to further their power of expression in music, allows them access to other types of music or arts related pastimes and introduces them to career possibilities in a field that interests and enthuses them.

Gifted and talented students

Music is used extensively with this group of students. It allows independent learning, the opportunity for students to develop at their own speed and to apply structure to their learning. Additionally the development of music introduces these students to complex concepts and processes. The process of bi-hemispherical thought, the creative combined with the logical/mathematical, is a significant aspect of music that frequently serves the specific needs of gifted and talented students.

Whole-school creativity

Chorlton has just been re-designated as an 'Arts College' and one of its significant development targets is the promotion and use of creativity across the curriculum. Commitment to the use of the arts has not come overnight. Not surprisingly, at the outset of Arts College status there were members of staff who were unsure of what it meant and were unsure of how it might support learning. However, during the first four years of having Arts College status, the opportunity to see the benefits in action, along with natural staff turnover (which has brought in staff already committed to the idea), have combined to create a teaching force who have very much bought into the idea of learning through the arts.

This commitment has led to much greater involvement in creative partnerships projects across the curriculum and involvement with outreach projects based at local theatres or other arts organizations. One recent project has involved the humanities faculty joining forces with the Royal Exchange Theatre, thereby exploring curriculum themes through drama, dance and music.

However, while that is the sort of project that will attract attention it is in truth only a small part of the school's provision and this provision is frequently showcased in arts assemblies. All of the subject areas and groups involved in the arts have an opportunity to perform to their year group in the theatre, during an assembly. Not only does this cement the ethos of arts education among the students, it allows staff to see students in a different light and encourages them to appreciate, and subsequently adopt, different approaches to the teaching of their subject.

This raised awareness of arts opportunities within the curriculum has acted as an agent of Continuing Professional Development (CPD) and teachers from non performing arts faculties are now initiating their own arts related programmes.

One of the most recent projects inspired by this process is being carried out by the modern languages department. Specifically a teacher of French, supported by a grant from Creative Partnerships, is working with a musician to create, with the students, songs in French about bullying.

Zoë Morris is convinced that one of strengths of music in the curriculum is the wide range of its appeal, variety of styles and potential applications. Chorlton High has just launched a TV station and one of the criteria when forming the board of directors was the inclusion of students with a wide range of musical interests so that R&B, funk, rap, indie, classical and so on would all be represented. Thus the process is differentiated, not by musical ability, but through musical tastes and opportunity. Such an approach is not only desirable in educational terms (differentiation by outcome is *not* seen as the way forward at Chorlton) but also in socio-economic terms, since it reflects the wide range of backgrounds from which the student population is drawn.

As Zoë puts it, when she first came to the school there was a lot of 'glockenspiel' behaviour, largely for the convenience of the teachers, and not a great deal of work that sought to embrace the diversity of the school population.

The approach of the music department is now one of exploring, performing and appreciating world music. Additionally, though more recently, music technology has assumed more significance. At first technology was introduced as part of the 'music makers' inclusion project. A group of disaffected Year 9 boys worked each Friday morning with a DJ and a film maker. The initiative sparked so much enthusiasm that by Year 10 the boys were offered and readily accepted the chance to pursue a National College of Further Education (NCFE) award, equivalent to two GCSEs. Though not normally available in schools special permission was obtained through the Special Schools' Trust and a number of arts colleges now offer a similar course.

The entire original group passed the course in 2006. Not only did these students re-engage with education in music, they re-engaged with school and achieved qualifications in other curriculum areas. Indeed, far from failing to complete their formal education, in a number of cases they chose to go on to college. From this 'alternative curriculum pilot' the course has now been offered to the whole student cohort and has been so successful that it is, in truth, proving too popular in resource terms.

Making music successful

The staff at Chorlton High share the view that in order to make music successful it is vital to be clear about its purpose. Furthermore that purpose can only be recognized if the diversity of the subject is recognized. In a great many schools music is still invested with the sole purpose of being a promotional tool. The minority of students, and it almost always is a minority, are wheeled out like circus animals to perform on open evenings and so on. Clearly there is a place for the high achievers and inevitably there will be a tension between provision for the elite and inclusion but Zoë Morris is unequivocal when she says: 'It is possible, and of paramount importance, to cater for both.'

As with all subjects music has an intrinsic value but in the past that intrinsic value has been defined by value judgements based on what teachers thought to be 'worthy'. Morris says: 'At Chorlton we see it as vital to be up to speed with the pupils, and not vice versa.'

If music is approached from this direction then not only can the needs of every type and level of musician be accommodated, but music can also 'pay back' the investment by equipping students with skills and concepts that will be transferable to other areas of the curriculum and by helping them to engage both academically and socially.

Thus it is that Chorlton High makes a conscious effort to provide for all needs and tastes. In the case of choral singing for example there are two choirs in the school; one for anyone who wants to sing and the other for those with particular skills who are able to deal with more demanding genres and arrangements. In the vast majority of cases the students are able to judge for themselves where they should be and, should this not be the case, then the skill of the teacher is there to guide them.

Morris states: 'Differentiation should come through a broad range of opportunities not through outcome.' On that basis she finds no difficulty in justifying the school's karaoke club, pointing out that something that originated by student request as an after-school club has now proved to be an invaluable gateway for the introduction of singing, confidence, teamwork and decision making in music lessons.

The provision of a broad range of opportunities is further vindicated by the fact that it gives immediate and clear support to major parts of the school's equal opportunities and ethnicity policies. Demonstrably in the school this wide range of opportunities gives the students a much more inclusive view of what achievement is and causes them to be far more receptive to new ideas.

In addition to the variety of curricular and extra-curricular activities the school also supports an extensive peripatetic programme. The scheme takes place during the school day, with students being released from lessons. The scheme is monitored very closely, not least because the students pay but more significantly, from a budgetary point of view, because the school provides a subsidy for the scheme based on factors such as instrument, group size and school meal entitlement.

Zoë is convinced that the importance of music at Chorlton means that students leave school with that little bit 'extra' that they can carry with them into the future. School is not just about lessons and the National Curriculum. It is equally important in developing the individual, and participation in music is a major factor in unlocking social skills, friendships, confidence, self-esteem and a host of other skills that will equip students for life.

Shropshire County Council music service

A qualified teacher since 1976 and an advisor with Shropshire County Council since 1997, Keith Havercroft now holds the post the post of Schools Improvement Advisor (Music and E learning) and is responsible for the excellent website 'music for teachers' (www.m4t.org).

Importantly for Keith his role as advisor to schools operates in tandem with another – that of head of the county instrumental music service. While it is true that some authorities run the services independently, Keith feels that an instrumental teaching service cannot be separated from the whole-school curriculum. Thus, in his view, it has been an advantage to have the two combined, allowing an integrated provision.

The instrumental service has changed markedly under Keith's leadership. It was originally solely an instrumental service and those instruments were, without exception, orchestral. While the service continues to offer orchestral tuition it also now offers voice and pop tuition, coupled with a broader curriculum support, allowing it to work with a more diverse range of students.

The increased diversity means that the number of students that the service works with has doubled. The greatest increase has come in drum kits, electric keyboards, guitars and electric bass. The service now runs more than 20 ensembles of the classical, jazz, wind band and swing band variety as well as keyboard and guitar ensembles.

Over the years Keith and his staff have experimented with a variety of ways to offer new music opportunities to the young people of the county. Some have worked; some haven't.

Promoting change is, in itself, easy, says Keith. The important thing is in recognizing whether the new venture is actually achieving the required objectives and accepting that some projects will fall short of the targets. The key, says Keith, is not to view this shortfall as failure but as a positive thing. 'Provided that any project is accompanied by a balanced evaluation, even if it is informal, then the positives can be retained and those organizing it can use it as a basis for future improvement.'

One recent example of development has been the introduction of a new orchestra. While Keith is in no doubt that orchestras, like the Shropshire Youth Orchestra, are a 'wholly good thing' he does agree that for some young musicians, and possibly the audience, their repertoire can become somewhat stilted. Since replacing it was never an option Shropshire have introduced, in conjunction, the Shropshire Pops Orchestra, the aim of which is to play contemporary film score.

Whenever a 'blockbuster' film comes out the music service immediately seeks permission to arrange and perform the score and to add it to their repertoire. The orchestra meets just three times a year and stages a big charity concert at which they play a maximum of eight big film scores.

The success of the project, and it has been a big success, has been the fact that the music is often well known to the performers and therefore very motivating. It is a change of style for those already in the Youth Orchestra and it gives an opportunity to some types of instruments that would not normally see themselves included in the Youth Orchestra. The music says Keith is 'as demanding as a symphonic score' but, because the score is bigger than its symphonic counterpart, it allows for the inclusion of extended percussion, a larger bass section, double the woodwind and so on.

In a break from the normal protocol, the practice is that a different person conducts each piece. The result has been that the orchestra now consists of more advanced student performers playing alongside adults, who are a mix of schoolteachers, music service teachers and members of the community. Through this arrangement the students gain invaluable experience and are able to see that music can be a lifelong pursuit and pleasure. For their part the community, whether as audience or performers, are able to see at first hand what goes on in school and some of the benefits that can be derived from studying and performing music.

The key to the success and diversity of musical opportunities in Shropshire is that none of the activities is over demanding in terms of time commitment. Performances are limited to one per term, the only exception being when an ensemble is raising money to fund a tour. None of the concerts is over rehearsed. In Keith's opinion young musicians need fresh challenges and their enthusiasm can be dampened if they spend too long with one piece. That is not to say that standards are compromised and the performers know when they attend full rehearsals that the time they have spent in private rehearsal will be invaluable.

The teamwork that underpins performance is, in Keith's view, an important aspect of studying and making music. For this reason he is always keen to combine it with other subjects and art forms, encouraging performers to play at art exhibitions or for drama and dance performances. In the same way the staff are encouraged to adopt and promote the same approach. A violin teacher, for example, is expected to know what is going on across the board in the teaching of music, not just in their narrow area.

The logistics of rehearsals

In a widespread and lightly populated authority like Shropshire transport is one of the major problems when it comes to organizing rehearsals. As Keith says: 'Without transport problems the numbers taking part would double.'

One solution is to have a variety of ensembles available. Some of those are locally based and are designed to provide experience for those beginning in music. Others, based in Shrewsbury because it is roughly central, attract more experienced players from across the county.

In theory the admission to ensembles is by audition but in practice, since they are designed to support students and their interests, no one is ever turned away. The music service is proud to take the view that if someone is prepared to give up time to make music then there will always be an appropriate opportunity for them.

For the local ensembles transport is pretty straightforward and is usually taken care of by the parents. For the Shrewsbury based ensembles the music service has simply had to accept the cost implications and provides five coaches from different compass points. While the coaches are by no means full, without them the county ensembles simply couldn't function.

Funding

In order to carry out its diverse activities the Shropshire music service has to draw funds from a variety of different sources.

- central government standards fund
- county council finance

122

- income from Schools' Service Level Agreements (SLA)
- charges for lessons (more than the combined amount from others sources)
- Shropshire Youth Music Parents and Helpers Organization (SYMPHO)
- front of house/ticket sales/other sources.

Ticket sales are not a huge amount because the music service has adopted a policy of low admission prices, even for some of their largest events. Although £10 per ticket would be realistic, an average price of about £4 is charged in recognition of the fact that the audience is largely made up of family members and they have, in a sense, already paid by financing lessons, instrument purchase, giving up time, using their cars and so on.

The money that SYMPHO raises is extremely useful in that it pays for new scores and keeps the repertoire fresh. It subsidizes any pupils who may need financial support and perhaps, most importantly, it gives a significant role to parents, recognizes their contribution and maintains their involvement.

Supporting students

Any support that a student needs is administered in a completely anonymous way. Only one officer from the music service is aware of who receives support. All applications go to him, cheques from SYMPHO are paid to his budget heading and only he is aware of who receives the money. Naturally the process is audited in line with public sector standards but Keith and all those involved are insistent that this is the best and the only system that should be used.

The central government standards fund (England)

In the late 1990s various people associated with the arts became aware that insufficient was being spent on that area of the curriculum. Indeed some authorities were economizing to the extent that they were disbanding their music services. Not surprisingly this prompted significant discussion and a number of music celebrities and a government working party combined to seek a solution. The result was the 'standards fund'– a tranche of money earmarked for a specific purpose, in this case music.

The amount of money set aside was insufficient to entirely finance the provision of music in local authorities but when placed alongside existing funding it made a significant difference. It is true that some authorities, faced with different financial priorities, used the money to replace existing provision and in that sense it brought no more 'to the table'. However, there is now a guarantee that some music provision will exist in all local authorities because the standards fund has to be spent on that area of the curriculum. However, this particular arrangement applies in this form only in England. Teachers in Wales, Scotland and Northern Ireland are advised to familiarize themselves with the specific regulations that apply to their region.

The cost of the music service

The Shropshire music service, in common with its counterparts in many parts of England and some other areas of the UK, has to balance its books by providing specific services at a cost effective and economically viable rate. Thus it is that although some provision might appear to be free and some appears to be charged for, in truth everything is costed out at a rate of £50 per hour. The funds raised can be used to subsidize some initiatives but most have to be self-financing. There are those who refer to the past and point out that everything in those days was free but they are, at best, guilty of selective recall. While it is true that it was less likely that music support for schools was charged for in the past, it is equally true that funds were finite and whatever provision there was could only be offered to a favoured few.

Nowadays the provision is more evenly available and schools are able to learn for themselves how to set up, buy in and finance music programmes. The result is that there is greater diversity of provision than in the past and because schools have a financial stake in the projects they tend to have greater longevity.

Cost to parents in Shropshire

Music lessons for all instruments are provided throughout the school year in Shropshire. In total there are usually 32 lessons, costing £7.40 per lesson, leading to a total cost of £236.80. The price remains the same whatever the format of the lesson. For example, four beginners would each pay £7.40 for a group lesson of 30 minutes, while a more advanced student would pay the same for 20 minutes of individual tuition. In Keith Havercroft's experience this pricing structure is easily understood by parents, they know where they are up to financially and the students have a chance to progress. The teachers for these lessons are not necessarily fully qualified schoolteachers with PGCE Qualified Teacher Status (QTS) or Bachelor of Education degrees (BEd). They can also be qualified and/or experienced professional musicians who have the skill to teach and the musical ability to inspire and motivate students.

Membership fees

All of the ensembles and music events that the music service provides are organized under the umbrella of the Shropshire School of Music and students are charged a membership fee to participate. Regional ensembles are charged at the rate of £20 per term and the county ensembles at the higher rate of £32 per term. On the face of it this seems expensive and it is true that the cost of lessons, membership fees and instrument purchase do mount up. On the other hand, when compared to the cost of other activities such as football, tennis, cricket, Cubs, Brownies and so on, and the cost of kit, coaching schools, uniform, camps and so forth the costs are not comparable.

The music service, says Keith, tries to provide what schools cannot. Not many schools can sustain a full orchestra and even if they do other pressures mean that rehearsals are sometimes cancelled. The music service never cancels and has put into place a system of substitute facilitators who step in at very short notice to cover things like sudden illness. In this way parents and performers never feel let down and are able to feel that they are getting value for money. In the same way, the service has been able to create a bank of instruments that can be loaned and has negotiated very favourable rent/buy schemes with local music shops.

Age groups for instrumental ensembles

At the upper end the cut off for those participating is usually the age at which students leave school and move on to work, further education or higher education. However since the provision is run by the music service, rather than by the schools, there is no upper age cut off since membership is open to any Shropshire resident.

Equally there is no official lower age limit. The right to participation is decided on the basis of a child's ability to cope both musically and socially. The music service does do work with pre-school children, mainly through the 'mini-strings initiative'. The choice of violins as the main instrument is due entirely to the fact that they are made full size, three-quarter size, half size and so on, whereas other instruments such as flutes are of fixed proportions and require a certain hand span to use the keys. In the case of younger children the music service allows open access to rehearsals for their carers. Having said all of that, Keith is not personally in favour of pupils learning any instrument from too young an age. Pupils cannot make real progress until their motor skills are sufficiently developed so starting too young can be a demotivating experience. Nevertheless if there is genuine interest he has no objection and, since the music service is a business, it responds to demand otherwise 'parents will go elsewhere'.

Problems facing music teachers in primary schools

While it is true that in the UK music is a statutory part of the curriculum there are in, some cases, problems with its provision. The core curriculum, Standard Assessment Tests (SATs) where they exist and the effect of league tables have, says Keith, combined to encourage in a significant number of headteachers and governors the belief that to be successful they must concentrate their resources on certain things. Often music is not high on that list of 'certain things'. Although many schools have recognized the problem and have made a deliberate policy to promote all of the arts, the pressures on teachers are tremendous and when viewed nationally there is undoubtedly a problem.

Subject specialism at primary level is also a consideration and some teachers believe that without that specialist knowledge they will be unable to teach the subject. Keith Havercroft does not share that view and is certain that with good support people motivated to teach music, although not good musicians themselves, can actually enable young learners to make good progress.

Often it is easier for the non-specialist to use the pupils' ideas without feeling that they need to impose their own and the result is therefore a more genuine piece of child-centred composition. Keith is in no doubt when he says: 'While it is important to have confidence it is not a problem if a primary school teacher cannot play the piano. The only thing that is a problem is a narrow understanding of who can and can't compose.' He goes on to say: 'Composition is not the sole province of dead Germans. Composition is about putting sounds into patterns and on that basis a teacher and a pupil can do it in the same way they that they can create a tessellation or a piece of art without the teacher being a mathematician or a trained artist.'

Resources are often a problem in the primary school and the limitations of, for example, an open-plan building can be intimidating, not just because the teacher is aware that a lively music lesson may disturb colleagues' quieter teaching but also because the less confident teacher may feel on show in such a situation. In such circumstances staff have to be clear and united in their philosophy of music teaching and must be supported by well-planned schemes and adequate training, so that they can draw strength from the knowledge that each knows what the other is doing and all know what they are attempting to achieve for their pupils.

This shared understanding and philosophy combine to reduce the pressure, present in some schools, to achieve an 'outcome'; something that can be performed either in class or at the school concert. This demand, as well as ignoring the importance of the processes of teamwork and investigation, also imposes a value judgement upon the music by suggesting that composition has to have a 'right answer' and is only worthy if it fits a narrow preconception of what good music actually is.

If a performance is required then teachers should not be afraid of work in progress. They should have a confidence and a pride in what the pupils have produced and should make it accessible to the audience by acquainting them with the process and context in which the music was created.

Helping pupils to compose

In giving pupils the opportunity to make music or to compose there are, in Keith's view, certain essential elements that the teacher must put in place. Of central importance is lots of good teaching about how to do things. It is wrong, says Keith, to give pupils instruments and expect them to produce something. You have to model and demonstrate, either personally or through recorded examples, so that pupils have a framework. At first this may result in pupils producing something similar to the teacher's example but subsequently, when they are free to 'do their own thing' they will be armed with techniques that they can apply in new situations. Keith is very clear about this when he says: 'Without technique pupils will never progress.'

This belief in technique is Keith's reason for focusing so strongly on learning objectives on his website. He firmly believes that teachers have to be clear about the order of things they need to be teaching. He says: 'Without that framework you may just as well give the pupils resources and let them play with them and see what they come up with.' The natural consequence of that approach, however, would be to differentiate by outcome and in doing so the pupils who need more support are neglected.

Why is composing so important?

Composing is a process whereby lots of quite simple components, lots of bits of understanding and skills are taken, reordered and combined into a much more complex whole. It is in fact synthesizing and in Bloom's *Taxonomy of Learning* (1984) synthesis is one of the higher-level thinking skills.

In music, indeed in all of the arts when we are creative, we are involved in the process of making complex things out of simple things. It is in fact higher-order thinking. The three areas that Bloom identifies as part of that process of higher-order thinking are:

- analysis (understanding how it works)
- synthesis (creating what we want)
- evaluation (not marking but genuine qualitative judgement).

Evaluation in the above sense means a true critique of each other's work. One of the problems that many people have with the presence of the arts in the curriculum is one of assessment. How, they ask, do you mark them without being subjective? The question is asked and invites the inference that marking somehow makes a subject superior. In truth it is evaluation that is the more rigorous process. Being awarded a mark out of 10 may tell you what you have got right but it does nothing to help you with what you have got wrong.

The element of evaluation within composing enhances peer and self-assessment so that children actually get answers to questions like 'How have I succeeded?' or 'What can I do to improve?' In doing so they can recognize where they are, where they want to be and what targets they must set to move on.

Our view of teachers

In the past our view of teachers was different. A good teacher had to 'know their stuff' and had to 'be good at what they did'. Thus the good music teacher had to know almost everything about music and had to be 'a good player'. Nowadays, knowledge and skills are not enough. Indeed, and this is particularly true with pupils or less experienced colleagues, by knowing too much we can intimidate people to the extent that they are unable to emulate the teacher's skills from the outset. Alternatively it may be that a teacher knows so much and are so adept that they lose sight of the challenges that certain tasks and skills present.

What we expect nowadays is a teacher who 'can do' and 'does know' but of equal (and some might say greater importance) is the skill to inspire confidence in pupils and to instil a desire to take the subject further.

Coordinating music in the primary school

The good music coordinator in the primary school must do all of the above but must take it one step further in that they must also instil confidence in those colleagues who are non-specialists in the teaching of music. In doing this, says Keith, it is no good going to colleagues and showing them lessons that they can't replicate. If they can't play the piano then your use of the instrument won't help them. If, on the other hand they can use backing tapes then that is the resource that must be made available and that is what sample lessons and a scheme of work must be built around.

Most teachers, especially in primary schools, can to some extent teach almost anything. Music, however, is one of the subjects that they worry about. The reason for this is not simply that it is creative and requires technique. It is as much to do with the historical practice that has built up around it. Within a classroom the resources required for art often surround teachers and pupils. The resources required for drama and improvisation are equally accessible. It is not unusual for a teacher to set drawing as an extension task or to suggest that children should work in a group and decide what happened next. What is more unusual, despite the presence of instruments in a classroom, is the suggestion that children should extend their work through a music-making exercise. If the rooms and resources were available to do such a thing then the process of music making would become much less of a performance and teachers, specialist and non-specialist alike, would feel less under scrutiny when making music with the children.

Problems in secondary schools

The biggest problem facing schools throughout the UK is the shortage of specialist teachers available to deliver every aspect of the secondary curriculum. When this shortage of teachers is combined with the pressures of the National Curriculum it is easy to see why some schools construct timetable systems that limit access to music. The most common of these is the 'carousel system' up to Key Stage 3 (Year 9), a process that involves the students splitting into groups and spending a block of time, perhaps half a term, in each of the creative areas rather than a whole school year in each. While such a system allows some experience of music it does not necessarily provide the breadth required and is often followed by an option system for Key Stage 4 (Years 10 and 11) that *a*) reflects the partial experience of music up to that point and *b*) creates reduced choices ensuring that demand doesn't outweigh staff availability. It is also true that given the opportunities for learning and playing music outside school and the pressures, in some areas, created by school league tables, there is a genuine temptation on the part of some teachers to form examination groups based upon those pupils who are already adept and talented rather than creating truly mixed ability groups. At the same time parents themselves, aware of curricular demands and career prospects might be tempted to discourage the choice of music in the belief that it will not lead to a 'real' job and that it can, in any event, be pursued as a hobby.

In some schools staffing issues have, in part, been addressed by the introduction of performing arts courses. While such a policy offers some opportunity to be involved in music there is a school of thought, worthy of note, that suggests that such courses dilute the music experience available, reducing the need to read music or to play to any standard, thereby failing those students who need or would prefer a more rigorous music syllabus.

Given the problems outlined at KS4, the retention at KS5 of more conventional A level or higher level examinations is in itself fraught with difficulty. Speaking about the English system Keith Havercroft is clear in his view when he states that the A level system is 'something of a dinosaur'. When GCSE was introduced and changes including the introduction of composition came about, no equivalent changes were made to A level. The end result now is that A level music is rather like a watered down degree course rather than a logical extension to GCSE music. Secondary teachers need to ask, bearing in mind what students might want to do in the future, whether a pure A level course is appropriate. In its present form, although useful to skilled musicians who want to pursue a course, it is not necessarily ideal for those wishing to become a performer or to be involved in the wider music business. In those circumstances music technology may be a better option. Through that route young musicians can become aware of more contemporary ways of making music. Such knowledge doesn't mean that contemporary music is all that can be performed. It merely means that the course offers modern approaches to a vast range of music in a way that engages young people and serves their needs.

Among many who continue to promote only the traditional A level approach there persists a view that it can only be 'musically legitimate' if it is classical. In truth, there exists a plethora of music, classic rock, jazz, Blues and so on that has stood the test of time, merits analysis and is far less alien than some of the more esoteric musical forms rooted in the seventeenth and eighteenth centuries. If, says Keith, we are to study a range of music across a variety of cultures, thereby addressing the needs of the modern school population, there has to be a spread and there is not a spread when 90 per cent of the pieces included for study on a syllabus are orchestral pieces from the classical romantic period.

Where can teachers find support?

The days when advisors popped in and out of schools to offer support, advice and to demonstrate new techniques have now largely gone. Most authorities throughout the UK do offer some sort of advisory service but, as indicated above, there is usually a cost implication for schools. From an advisor's point of view this often means that they are called in only when a problem has developed and from the school's point of view it often means that seeking external help with curriculum planning is, if not the last resort, then some way down the list. Knowing this is no help to the music coordinator and it is small comfort to hear that the government, local or national, has allocated money if, when the money is devolved to schools, it is swallowed up in the budget as a whole. Understandably schools, their management and governing bodies give priority to the core curriculum and subjects like music are sometimes seen as less important. The music coordinator must, therefore, be aware from the start that the search for support may be a difficult one. Nevertheless a continued effort to integrate music into the curriculum and a firm policy to make people aware of the benefits of creative education will eventually bring its rewards. In the meantime, and in the absence of more funding, the education departments of all the constituent countries of the UK have invested resources in the provision of advice, schemes of work and so on, on the internet. Keith Havercroft has himself been something of a pioneer in this field and is convinced that good quality websites can be an invaluable resource for teachers.

The 'music for teachers' website

Keith originally hit upon the use of the internet as a way of using modern technology to get into schools in a more efficient and cost effective way. Too often visits that schools are paying for involve the same baseline work on schemes, lesson planning and so on, before progress can be made. The development of the website has allowed Keith get information to teachers and has frequently removed the need for visits to the school. In addition the website, because of its accessibility, has allowed a consistent message to be communicated to all schools in the authority and coordinators, for their part, report that it gives invaluable support to the non-specialist and allows them to take consistent decisions in a more independent manner.

An additional success of the site has been the opportunity to share good practice on a national and even international basis. For some time it has been apparent to Keith that the website is accessed not just by Shropshire teachers but also by teachers throughout the UK and the English speaking world. It was this phenomenon that inspired the introduction of the 'blog', allowing teachers to share good practice and give feedback. Keith is happy for anyone to use and adapt materials off the site for their own purposes. He is keen to point out that giving away an idea is not like giving away a car. Even after the gift is made the idea is still there for the originator to use. It will come as no surprise to readers of this book to learn that Keith has found teachers to be extremely generous with their ideas and the addition of the blog has created a method by which the ideas can be further evaluated and developed.

A music coordinator

Jean Merrifield was the music coordinator at Beamont Infant School in Warrington for 16 years before retiring in 2006. Beamont is an average sized infant school in an area with a high level of social deprivation. The attainment of pupils on entry is well below the national average.

As well as being a fully qualified teacher, Jean has reached Grade 8 piano, but this wasn't a pre-requisite for the role. In her last Ofsted inspection before retirement Jean's music teaching and her role as music coordinator was judged as being excellent in the Ofsted criteria.

Jean often attended courses relating to her role as music coordinator; some of these were LEA courses but most she sought out herself. She states: 'While there are always courses available a coordinator can only be sure of finding the support relevant to their school by being proactive in their search for support and training.'

As the only musician in the school Jean was always required to play the piano for school assemblies and to organize the choice and rehearsal of music for school performances. While this might appear to be a burden it did give Jean the chance to select and prepare musical experiences that were both appropriate to the children's learning needs and appropriate to the expertise of her non-specialist colleagues.

On occasions Jean delivered specialist music lessons to all classes but also set up a programme of demonstrations and INSET that enabled other staff to deliver lessons. She introduced the use of ICT in music using programmes such as 'Compose World 2' and disseminated her knowledge to other staff to enable wider use of the software throughout the school. She also researched and introduced school-wide initiatives such as the playing of music to children at various times of the day.

Music was played in each classroom when the pupils arrived in the morning, which instilled a calm atmosphere and made sure the pupils were ready to learn. Jean also successfully experimented with playing classical music during activities such as handwriting practice. She found that the pupils' concentration greatly improved and they began to associate certain pieces of music with certain activities. Jean also investigated the use of music across the curriculum and began to use singing in maths lessons as a way of remembering times tables. These techniques were then transferred to other subjects.

Links with other schools were important at Beamont and teachers took children to perform in concerts at a local arts college and at the local high school. Jean also took a choir every year to take part in the local music festival, ensured that she was involved in LEA music meetings and organized regular visits from outside performers who gave follow up workshops to pupils and teachers.

Jean used the QCA music schemes as a basis for learning but commented that non-specialists found them hard to understand. This was mainly due to the use of subject specific vocabulary. She used the music attainment targets for pupils at the end of Key Stage 1. Jean monitored the provision in the timetable and ensured that all pupils received some music provision in the week. Sometimes this was limited to 30 minutes due to other curriculum demands.

The headteacher was extremely supportive of all music related activities and the important role of the coordinator. Time was allocated on a regular basis for Jean to fulfil her role. Other members of staff were appreciative of Jean's support and relied upon her expertise to satisfy the requirements of the National Curriculum.

Speech level singing

'Speech level singing' or SLS is a singing technique that enables the user to sing with power and expression over their whole vocal range. The technique enables singing to become as effortless as speaking. SLS involves the avoidance of tension in the outer muscles of the larynx. This prevents strain and damage to the vocal cords and can be applied to any style of music.

The technique was developed by Seth Riggs in response to the demands put upon the voices of professional singers. SLS technique allows performers to sustain long periods of rehearsal and performance without any vocal strain. His clients include over 120 Grammy award winners and numerous Academy Award winning actors.

SLS teachers have to undergo training and observation on a regular basis. Teachers are awarded different levels depending on their experience and training. The Liverpool Institute of Performing Arts or LIPA is the first university to be affiliated with SLS and use SLS teachers to deliver singing lessons to students.

There are currently less than 20 SLS certified teachers in the UK. Helen Monks is a level 1 teacher. She has been teaching singing for six years and has been applying the SLS methods to her teaching for two years. During the transition period in her teaching methods she noticed a remarkable difference in the results of the students she had been working with. She states: 'They instantly had more control over breaks and had less problems running out of breath. Many pupils have extended range which has given their confidence a boost.'

The confidence and self-belief that a teacher can inspire in their students is, in Helen's view, vital to their progress and their ability to achieve their true potential. Being a specialist teacher who comes in from outside the school environment enables Helen to form a different relationship with her students. Apart from having no axe to grind as far as the school's management is concerned, Helen is also able to form, within professional constraints, a different relationship with her students. To begin with, as a performer, they see her as an expert. In addition she can deal with them on a much more personal level and make their progress and her teaching much more of a partnership.

In addition to teaching singing, Helen performs on a regular basis. She comments on the difference SLS has made to her own voice: 'I find that I can concentrate on the interpretation of songs now that I don't have to worry about reaching difficult notes.' Helen feels that the teaching of singing in this way has undoubted benefits for her students.

What can we learn from these examples?

Although the work done in each of the exemplar cases differs quite considerably, all of those quoted have achieved similar objectives and all of them have observed certain protocols in the delivery of music. It is these protocols that are most readily transferable to other situations and which provide valuable guidance to teachers and managers alike.

Creating a distinctive curriculum

In every case the teachers involved have tried to create a curriculum that makes their particular course or programme of study stand out as different. Courses should be designed to suit the needs of pupils, not the needs of individual teachers or school management structures. To this end, in the examples given music has grown to fit the demands and needs of the pupils, not to suit the requirements of teacher availability. As far as the pupils are concerned they are left feeling that they are taking part in something enjoyable that has been designed for them and on that basis are more likely to succeed both in music and in the wider curriculum.

Furthermore, by taking such an approach it is in consequence easier to provide an inclusive curriculum that addresses the needs of all from the least able, the disengaged and the gifted and talented.

Music is not elitist

In every case the music provided has been differentiated, not on the basis of outcome but on the basis of the pupils' needs. Pupils have been offered a variety of experiences and opportunities and only require a willingness to participate. Ability should not be the only criteria for access to a music course and neither should it be the sole means of judging success. Equally teachers are there to facilitate, not to preach. They should not impose their preferences or prejudices on learners. Karaoke sessions have their place and could prove to be as valuable a teaching tool as more traditional genres.

Pupils can learn from each other

While it is true that participation in music allows teachers to see pupils in a different light it is also true that it allows pupils to see their peers differently. Quite apart from developing their musical skills pupils also gain from the opportunity to mix with each other. The opportunity to work collectively on a piece of music or a performance improves pupils' self-esteem, their sense of well being, their tolerance and their understanding of others.

Staff can learn from each other

In the most successful music schemes all staff are encouraged to take part and are given the opportunity to develop their expertise. Irrespective of age group or subject area music is a valuable tool for assisting learning. Good music schemes provide ample opportunity for teachers to learn from INSET and by observing or working with colleagues in supportive, non-judgemental circumstances.

Not only teachers can teach

Pupils and their teachers can benefit enormously from working with music professionals, who have a passion and an expertise that they can communicate to young learners.

Music can build a community

Not only can music cement relationships among pupils, irrespective of year groups, it can also create a sense of belonging within schools. It can be used to forge links with other schools, can assist with transfer and can build a positive profile for school and education within a community. It can draw parents into schools, improve their interest in their child's education and help them to see how education really can be a home–school partnership.

10

GETTING QUALIFIED/ GETTING A JOB

Despite clear evidence of music's importance to the rest of the curriculum it is extremely important that we remember that it is a subject in its own right. Without wishing to minimize the importance of its contribution to other subjects, first and foremost music stands alone as an area of the curriculum that not only encourages and develops essential life skills but also as a subject that gives very real prospects of a rewarding and fulfilling career.

A career in music

For those keen on music there are available numerous courses, examinations and qualifications suited to a wide range of interests and abilities and these will be examined later in the chapter. However, irrespective of the academic route, there is one quality indispensable to those contemplating a career in music and that is passion.

Though impossible to quantify and lacking formal assessment criteria, without a passion for their subject it is virtually impossible for someone to progress and achieve success in the world of music.

Whatever the subject, students have to learn that to succeed at anything hard work and commitment have to be at the centre. However, if they have a passion for their chosen subject then they will also learn that hard work becomes far easier if it is linked to something that they enjoy. Better still, if it is linked to something that they love then hard work can even become pleasurable and the importance of passion in those circumstances needs no explanation.

When does a career start?

It is easy to fall into the trap of thinking that career decisions need only be made when a student is older. Indeed, with an increasing number of students entering further and higher education, it sometimes feels as if decisions are only taken when the learner reaches their early twenties. The reality is that these impressionistic views tell only part of the story and in truth decisions are taken far earlier. All primary school teachers worthy of their profession are keenly aware that the foundations that they lay are the start of the process and although not in themselves career decisions, they nevertheless make pupils aware of opportunities and choices. It is no exaggeration then to say that the seeds of a career may well be sown at a very early age and the opportunities we offer young learners may well shape their lives for ever.

Clearly this view is not one that can be applied exclusively to music and no one would argue that it should be. Nevertheless the hierarchy of subjects referred to elsewhere in the book undoubtedly exists and this, coupled with a lack of awareness of career opportunities in music, means that the subject is often treated as a side issue and students are encouraged to see it as a hobby rather than a serious career possibility.

Knowing the exact moment when a career starts is, in truth, not the important thing. What is crucial is the realization that a career may start at a very early age. What teachers have to be aware of, therefore, is that the opportunities that they offer cannot easily be replaced and thus they have a vital role to play, from the early years on, in ensuring that they are aware of career possibilities and that the choices that education should afford really are available.

Living in the real world

When young people declare that they want to make a career in music they are often told that it is a 'nice idea' but that they need to 'live in the real world'. If we stop to consider how much talent has gone undeveloped and how many lives have remained unfulfilled as a result of these well intentioned but misguided words then the answer could be, to say the least, a little disturbing.

There is nothing more natural than a parent or a teacher wanting to protect from disappointment those whom they respectively love or care for. However it is important to remember that care is an interactive process and real love and real education depend not upon compelling or stifling young people but on giving them choice. On that basis it is the responsibility of parents and teachers to get themselves into the real world and since parents so often look to them for guidance it is likely that it will be the teachers who are called upon to set the agenda and to take the lead.

Is there really a future in music?

When researching careers in music the briefest trawl of the internet reveals over 150 areas of work, more than 70 musical styles and a least 60 different instruments that a musician might play. Given this diversity of opportunity and the widely held view that the creative industries are central to the world's economy then we begin to see that the real world might well hold considerable promise for the aspiring musician.

Currently the UK music industry has a turnover of about £3 billion per annum and employs approximately 150,000 people. When considering this number it is worth comparing it to other established areas of employment. It is, for example, greater than the number of solicitors currently registered to practice in the UK and even the UK insurance industry, the third largest in the world, can only claim to employ slightly in excess of 300,000 people. There are obviously numerous examples but the fact remains that as an area of employment, although seen as peripheral, music bears comparison with other professions normally perceived to be more mainstream in terms of the opportunities available.

How do we help?

An important starting point when assisting aspiring musicians is the injection of a healthy dose of realism. That is not to say that we should discourage ambition but it does mean that we must ensure that ambition is based upon some element of rational thought and planning. Above all, students must not confuse a desire to be famous with a genuine ambition to follow a career in music.

Having a plan

Successful projects often start with a good action plan and the formulation of one when advising students has two advantages. In the first place it helps the teacher to gain a balanced overview of the possibilities and pitfalls associated with a particular career path and second it makes it more likely that through the research and planning process the student will gain impartial and effective advice. Having said that it is useful to remember that in any career unexpected opportunities present themselves along the way and, even with the best of plans, accidents (hopefully happy ones) can occur and directions can change. The plan then has to be flexible and all parties must see it as a working model, not a solid framework.

Does realism prevent dreams?

In short, there is nothing wrong with having a dream. We all have them and often they guide us and drive us on to achieve things. If we ignore our dreams or someone discourages them they have a tendency to come back and haunt us. Hopefully when that happens we can do something about it but if it turns out that we can't then an unresolved dream can be the source of much frustration and sadness.

Dreams are not fantasies

Although dreams are permissible as part of a career goal, fantasies are not. Most of us, at one time or another, let our minds wander into unlikely realms where we can imagine spending our multi-million pound lottery win, meet our celebrity hero, enjoy sporting triumph and so on. However, when we come back to Earth we see those moments for what they are – fantasies. In the same way we must ensure that the people we are advising are not deluding themselves by believing that a flight of fantasy could become reality.

On the one hand, while anything might be possible we have to be honest with students if they have an unrealistic view of their ability or prospects. In truth this is not usually very difficult because in most case students are adept at making an honest appraisal of their skills. Once they have done that and express an ambition to pursue a career in music we must make sure that they know that support will be available and that they are also aware of the amount of hard work, persistence and sacrifice that may be required to turn dreams into reality.

And if it doesn't work out?

Sometimes it just doesn't happen. Despite the best-laid plans, despite the hard work and the talent it may be that someone doesn't get exactly what he or she hoped for. Although that may prove to be disappointing in the short term, with time to reflect it may be a little easier to take. Whatever happens the skills and qualities that music engenders are transferable in almost any situation and even if the ideal job doesn't present itself the talent will always be there. In truth though, given the range of possibilities available in today's music industry, it's more than likely that an adequate alternative will be available and in the final analysis it is still better to have pursued a dream and compromised a little than to face a future wondering what might have been.

Qualifications

There are numerous music qualifications available in the UK and their suitability depends very much upon the needs of the individual. Broadly speaking they can be divided into two main areas:

- public examinations accessed through schools, colleges and universities

- examinations provided and administered by private music organizations.

Schools and colleges throughout the UK

The Qualifications and Curriculum Authority (QCA) in England, the Scottish Qualifications Authority (SQA), the Council for the Curriculum, Examinations and Assessment (CCEA) in Northern Ireland and the Department for Education, Lifelong Learning and Skills in Wales all validate and supervise public examinations in their respective countries. Although each of the bodies differ in their exact remits the examinations that they oversee, although offered by a variety of examination boards, are substantially the same and have a large degree of parity.

The most widely known of the examinations are usually taken at the end of statutory education in the UK (15–16 years of age) and can be followed by higher level or A level examinations, often at around 17–18 years of age.

This major group of examinations is supplemented by a range of certificates, diplomas, vocational education certificates, national awards and higher national awards, covering areas such as performance and practice, production, musical theatre and technology and composition.

It is important to remember that although many of these qualifications have parity, they can differ considerably in their level and content. These differences are important when choosing courses of study appropriate to a particular student cohort and will also be important to parents and students when they choose institutions or programmes of study. Since the examination boards and supervisory bodies change and update examinations on a regular basis it is essential that those involved in music examinations, whether as teachers or learners, regularly check what the examination boards have to offer.

Parallel systems

Within the UK there has for some time been a debate about the relative merits of the 'academic' versus the 'vocational' route in education. The debate continues to be unresolved and despite the efforts of successive British governments to bring the two sides together there remain those firmly convinced that the one route is practically and/or intellectually superior to the other. We have no desire to enter into that debate and fortunately have no need to. Within the world of music the two systems have for a long time worked comfortably hand in hand. There are available, through public and private examination boards, qualifications that equip musicians with a range of practical and theoretical skills that are vital to the pursuit of their chosen careers.

Whatever the type, each is accepted as qualification for further courses or employment in the world of music. Often both types of qualification are required. On that basis, therefore, teachers should bear in mind that often it is the diversity of experience and qualification that equips the musician for the next stage in their career and on that basis alone those advising and teaching young people must ensure that the widest range of opportunities is available to the aspiring musician and put aside any preconceptions that they may have about the 'traditional', the 'practical' and the 'academic'.

University courses

Once students have taken courses at school or college they may wish to pursue a course at university. While it is not essential to have formal qualifications to pursue some careers in music, it is certainly desirable in some areas and in others it is essential. Further information on this is included later in Appendix A. Application for a degree course at a UK university has to be done through the Universities Central Admissions System (UCAS). All of the relevant information is available online at www.ucas.com. Applications can also be made online.

Music examinations through private organizations

Within the UK there exists a variety of organizations providing grading tests in music. The best among these are nationally recognized and are scrutinized by the qualifications and assessment authority for the country in which they operate. The qualifications that they offer are accepted by educational establishments and throughout the industry as standardized evidence of competence in music. Principal among them are the Associated Board of the Royal Schools of Music, the London College of Music and Trinity College, London. In reporting their existence we make no recommendation other than to say that all of them are nationally and internationally recognized.

The largest among them in terms of graded music examinations, the Associated Board of the Royal Schools of Music (ABRSM) reports on its website that:

> Over 620,000 candidates take our music exams each year in more than 90 countries around the world. We also run professional development courses for teachers and ABRSM Publishing publishes a wide range of repertoire, music books and CDs ... You can take exams in over 35 instruments, singing, jazz, music theory and practical musicianship ... Associated Board practical exams provide a progressive system of assessments beginning with the Prep Test and moving up through 8 grades to diplomas. They are designed to motivate pupils and students at all levels by providing clear attainable goals. The 'grades' are recognised as international benchmarks and are valued by teachers and institutions all over the world.

All of the boards provide similar services including help and advice on qualifications, teaching resources and advice for teachers and parents. If a student wants to pursue the study of music as a performer or teacher they will at some point be required to demonstrate their ability. The usual requirement is Grade 5 or above in these graded tests. Since specific requirements alter according to the individual, care should be taken to do the research and ascertain which tests will be required and what level will be expected.

Careers in music

As indicated previously, the music industry in the UK is a huge enterprise and although competitive there are opportunities for those who are determined to succeed. Add to the host of jobs available in music those jobs in related industries such as theatre, events management, education and so on, and the opportunities to use music in connection with your employment increases still further.

Practical steps for getting a job in music

We have already said that a passion for the subject is a central prerequisite for a career in music and it does no harm to repeat that advice. Students and their parents will often see a teacher as the first port of call when they are looking for help. Although teachers are not careers advisors there are general suggestions that they can make. As for the individuals, assuming that the passion is there, then there are a number of practical things that they can do to improve their chances of gaining employment in the music industry.

Practice

Whatever the area of interest there is no substitute for practice. Singers need to sing, instrumentalists need to play and composers should write as much as possible. If a particular area of interest involves recording, editing, mixing and so on, the same applies. There is no substitute for actually 'doing it'.

Research

Know your subject. Be aware of the courses you can take, get to know the technology that's available, be aware of different styles and musical genres and find out what jobs are available. You can never know enough and when you go for that all important interview or audition the hard work will be apparent and it will serve you well.

Get education, advice and training

Some people leave school at 16, get a break and follow a smooth and unobstructed career path from then on. For the most part however, while these people do exist they are the exception rather than the rule and the overnight success that we hear of is more often a myth created by the media. The simple fact is that there is no substitute for a good education allied to appropriate training. This route, conventional though it may be, ensures good knowledge, provides good experience and, over time, builds up the network of contacts that will be essential to success.

Believe in yourself

Don't be afraid to knock on doors. No one will do it for you. If you really want to succeed in music you must be prepared to seek out the opportunities. Unfortunately you must be prepared to receive more rejections than acceptances and to deal with them you have to believe in yourself or the difficulties you face will prove too hard to bear.

Work experience

There's no pay for this but it is a good way of getting experience and it looks great on a CV. Even though you are working for nothing you will still need to show determination or you won't get the placement. Remember a face to face request is often harder to refuse and persistence can bring rewards, so be cheeky. Work experience may not be a job but it may be the thing that finally gets you a job.

Look for relevant opportunities

If you want to be a performer, perform. Join a band, form a band, sing in a choir, play in an orchestra. If you want to write and compose, then do it. Everything that you do makes the next thing better. If sound mixing or being a DJ is what you want then remember that most hospitals have a radio station, as do many colleges and universities. Although they only have a restricted service licence (RSL) they do offer valuable experience. In the same vein the internet is a goldmine of opportunities for aspiring composers and performers with all the 'shop window' opportunities it offers in film making, community channels and showcase websites.

Don't expect to earn a fortune

While it's true that the rewards for some in the music industry are quite literally fabulous the truth is that most musicians do not move in those circles. Within the music industry a shrewd guess would put about 90 per cent of the wealth in the hands of about 2 per cent of the people. The starting point for working in music has to be the love of music. For those in search of fame there are almost certainly easier ways to gain it. For those in search of fortune, property speculation or a career on the stock market probably carries more guarantees. While an income of £50,000 pounds a year might ultimately be possible for some musicians it is worth remembering that starting money in some fields can be as low as £8–10,000 per annum and can involve regular periods of unemployment. By all means have ambitions but remember you're in this for the music and to have that and make a good living (as many do) is success in itself and brings more rewards than just a pay packet.

People skills

Remember that in many jobs related to music you are dealing with people who also feel passionately about their work. Although some would dismiss them as temperamental it is important to understand that their work is often very precious to them. Bearing that in mind you will have to be aware that as well as your music skills you will have to develop good people skills to deal with the difficult professional and social situations you will sometimes encounter.

So where are the jobs?

For those seeking further information about employment in the music industry more specific information can be found in Appendix A.

11
STAGING A PERFORMANCE

The upside

A school production or concert can often be a real highlight in the year for students, teachers and parents alike. It is a chance to show off all that is best about the school in particular and the education process in general. By joining together students from different year groups and teachers from different disciplines and then inviting the wider community to watch, a school performance demonstrates perfectly the importance and the nature of the education partnership. It gives students a chance to shine at a level appropriate to their needs and it gives them a chance to grow emotionally and to become aware of what they can achieve through hard work and careful preparation. At the same time it gives parents, teachers and peers the opportunity to see individuals in a new light and to appreciate talents that might not be so apparent in day-to-day situations.

The downside

The good news is that there is no reason why there should be a downside to any school performance. When all said and done it would be difficult to find anyone who would want it to fail and, given the personal involvement that most of the audience will have, they are likely to be positive in their reaction no matter what happens. However, it does not mean that things can't go wrong and neither does it mean that there is any substitute for careful planning and preparation. Like any other part of the curriculum a performance needs to be carefully planned and teachers and students need to be aware of what the outcomes should be and what constitutes an 'acceptable' standard.

The role of senior management

Senior mangers have a vital and very difficult role to play when school performances are being planned. Naturally they want to promote their school but their responsibilities are far wider than that. It is vital that at every stage they provide support for all of the staff and students involved. The expectations that they place upon them must be carefully judged. Too little and there will be no opportunity for staff and students to reveal their true potential; too much and performers will lose confidence and staff will become so stressed that their work in other areas could well suffer.

Choosing the project

The golden rule when deciding what sort of performance to do is to make an audit of the experience and expertise available. If you are the only teacher who is prepared to get involved and the students have no previous experience it will probably be unwise to embark upon a full scale musical as a starting point. Smaller events will help staff and students find their feet. If a major production is your long-term aim you should approach it with a long-term plan.

Preparing the ground

One of the determining factors in planning for a musical production will be the age range of the school. In general, schools in the secondary sector tend to be larger and as a consequence are more likely to have more staff and the possibility of a wider range of expertise. Secondary schools also tend to have more equipment and more disposable funds. Naturally all of these factors will have to be considered when the style and scale of the performance are being decided. Addition-ally the age range of the school is likely to influence the choice of material. The existence of these factors does not mean that one type of school will produce better work than others. However, if they are ignored during the planning stage it will, in all likelihood, mean that compromises will have to be made at a later stage.

Having taken all of the above into account it will then be necessary to decide exactly what type and scale of performance will be appropriate for your particular school. It is always better to start small and grow. With careful management this need not take a long time but it will ensure that the ethos of performance will become embedded in the life of the school and that more and more teachers and students will gain confidence and experience.

Starting points

Performances in assemblies are a good way of involving large numbers of students and teachers. At first the length of the assemblies can be limited and teacher input can control the timing of the items presented. The performance aspect should be dealt with in a very low-key manner and the exercise should be thought of as sharing rather than showing. Although the distinction may seem slight it is one that will do much to divert pressure from students and teachers. If the subject matter is based around school topics or themes from PSHE there will be great scope for the students to create their own music. Some of the pieces might even be unfinished and this should be accepted as the norm. In other subjects we have no problem with showing work in progress and 'seeing where we are up to' so there is no reason to be afraid of taking the same approach in music.

Moving on

Once the students have become used to performing to their peers then it is a good idea to develop the process by inviting parents. At first it may be enough to have family assemblies but in truth most parents will find it easier to attend evening performances. At first these concerts can follow the same format as the assemblies with teachers (or students) explaining the themes and the creative processes involved. This informal approach has the benefit of relaxing the performers and allowing parents an insight into the work that their child is involved in at school. This sort of work has a place in any concert but as expertise is developed more sophisticated and better rehearsed pieces can be added, giving greater variety to the programme and allowing parents to see how progress is made.

The 'big one'

When schools feel ready to stage a more ambitious project they will find a wide range of material available. Many schools choose well-known musicals, some go for pieces devised and composed by the students, while others opt to buy in production packages. There are many of the latter now available through various educational publishers and they usually include backing tracks, rehearsal CDs and advice on staging. All of these choices have their merits and you must decide which one is suitable for your school. Whatever your decision remember that the final product is about the students, not about the preconceptions of adults. Whatever you choose, the students should be capable of performing it and able to enjoy it.

Staging your production

Before you even think of announcing that there will be a production you must do an awful lot of preparation and you must think very carefully about your chosen show. If you are to be the director then you must have a very clear idea about what you want to achieve. In you mind's eye you must have an idea about how the piece will look, what the characters will look like, how they will dress and so on. You should also have an idea about how they will deliver their songs and their lines. True, you will have other staff to help you with these things but they will look to you for the overall vision. Unless you give them that vision you will have a team of assistants going off in different directions and your production will have no artistic cohesion.

The budget

Knowing how much you have to spend will probably affect both your choice of production and its style. It is possible to reduce production costs but one thing you cannot avoid is the performing rights licence.

Performance rights

If you choose a production written by someone else it is quite likely that you will have to pay a fee before you are granted performance rights. Details of how to apply for these rights can normally be obtained through the publisher. It is advisable to apply well in advance, particularly with popular pieces since there are sometimes restrictions on the number of licences that will be granted at any one time in a particular area. Often when you are granted the licence you will be given the opportunity to hire a set of scripts and full copies of the score. It is illegal to perform without a licence and you are in effect stealing income from the writers. It is also illegal to photocopy scripts and scores and there are instances of schools being prosecuted for these offences. In general the fees are reasonable, especially for amateur productions, and breaking the law is never advisable.

Raising money

Creating performances on a shoestring budget is a stressful process and often results in mediocrity. While there is no reason to advocate extravagance it is important that the performers know that their work is valued and that you are able to spend adequate amounts in order to achieve a good standard. The benefits of a school production are well documented and the importance of music has already been outlined in previous chapters. Given these facts it is not unreasonable to expect the school to have some sort of heading in its budget for public performances. However, given the financial demands faced by most schools it is likely that you will need to raise other funds and this will be a key role for your marketing team.

Fundraising is something that teachers are often involved in and on that basis you should have no difficulty in finding a willing and able volunteer.

Ticket sales

This is likely to be your largest single source of income. Unfortunately it only appears at the end of the production process and is a projected, rather than a guaranteed, amount. In order to finance the production you will need to negotiate an advance from a source such as the school fund and secure an agreement that the source will cover any shortfall in the event that ticket sales are poor. Naturally this is an eventuality that you would hope to avoid so you must set your ticket prices carefully, well in advance, make a realistic income projection and ensure that your marketing team have a good sales and publicity strategy prepared.

Programme sales

On the night of the performance it is usually possible to sell programmes at a nominal price. It is important to remember that you will have printing costs and that not everyone will buy a programme. On that basis programmes are unlikely to add a large amount to your budget so it is often a good idea to think of boosting income through advertising or sponsorship.

Advertising or sponsorship

Among the parents of many schools there are often those who run their own businesses or who are associated with large commercial concerns in the locality. In many cases the smaller businesses will be happy to take out a small advertisement in the programme. Several such advertisements will provide valuable revenue. In the case of the larger concerns many have a community sponsorship fund. There may be a possibility that they will be prepared to make a donation, particularly if they have a community governor at the school or if your publicity team are able to obtain press coverage. Naturally any press coverage will have the added benefit of promoting the performance.

The parents' association

Many schools have an active parents' association and they are often prepared to give financial support to concerts and musical productions.

Merchandizing

One way of creating a buzz about a production is by printing and selling T-shirts to the crew, the performers and other school members. Advance sales help to publicize the production and others can be sold on performance nights, along with refreshments and raffle tickets. On a more cautious note it is important to remember that a sense of professionalism can add a great deal to any performance. On that basis it is important to remember that the production is central, particularly on performance nights, and the artistic integrity of the production shouldn't be compromised by the drawing of raffle tickets or the presence of too many sales stalls.

Getting started

Having chosen the right production it is time to assemble your production team. The exact number will vary according to the show but to start with you will need:

- director (you)
- musical director
- technical director (sound/lighting/special effects – might be more than one person)
- designer (might cover set, props and costume or each might be separate)
- set construction
- properties (making and procuring)
- costume (making and procuring)
- publicity/marketing/business management
- front of house.

Each of the above will assemble their own teams around them

and some should control that area on the night but you will also need at some point:

- stage manager and assistants
- prompt
- runners.

Once you have assembled your team it must be clear from the start that you are in charge. As director you should have decided, in advance, your timescale for the production and this, together with your artistic vision, must be passed on at the production meetings. As long as people know what is expected of them you should have no trouble. If, on the other hand, you are indecisive the timetable will slip, conflict will arise and everyone's job will become more difficult.

Casting

This is never easy. From your point of view the pressure is there to get the right person in each role. Even though you have your artistic plan in place there will still be difficult decisions. With the best will in the world you will disappoint somebody. The only thing you can do is to be clear about what you want and be honest with those you are dealing with. Fortunately in musicals there is often an opportunity for people to remain involved even if they don't get a leading role. It is often helpful to explain to students that missing out at an audition doesn't mean you have failed. If the director is looking for a tall Asian boy and you happen to be a small white female there is nothing you can do about it.

Rehearsals

Know from the start when these will take place and whom you will need. Always give people plenty of notice and make it clear that rehearsals are not optional.

Discipline

161

No team event will function without discipline and it must be there from the start. If people are not pulling their weight then they must go. Do not be afraid to 'lose' people. There will always be willing replacements and it is important that everyone is aware that the show and not the individual is the important thing. If the cast see that one or two performers are 'holding you to ransom' you will be unable to maintain discipline and will face increasing problems as the project progresses.

Make sure that your cast know exactly what is expected of them. Be strict about timekeeping, don't allow them into the wings or front of house during a performance. Always have a signing in sheet so you know who is missing. Insist that everyone arrives at least 35 minutes before curtain at every performance and let no one leave until all props, costumes and other materials have been reset when the curtain comes down.

Responsibility

As the performances approach more and more responsibility should shift from the director to the production team and the performers. Prior to the first night you should have a full technical rehearsal to check all entrances, exits, lighting, sound and so on. This should be followed by a full dress rehearsal, which should be exactly as the performance will be. Never fall for the old wives tale that a bad dress means a good performance – it is simply not true. Students need confidence. Preparing them badly is more likely to mean that they will perform badly. Inexperienced directors often tell their cast prior to a run of four performances that they have four chances to get it right. The truth is that a cast only ever has one chance to get it right because the audience changes every night and those from night one will have no interest in the fact that 'it all went well by night four'.

Summary

Do everything you can to minimize the pressure on all concerned. Concerts and musical productions should be happy, show piece occasions for the school. Avoid turning the students into a sideshow attraction or a marketing tool. Performances should form part of a broad and balanced education for the students, in line with national requirements and standards. Somewhere along the way, as part of a process not unrelated to parental choice and league tables, concerts have become competitive and the standards by which they are judged have become increasingly adult rather than child centred. The answer to this would seem to be to educate parents as well as students. The purpose of music is not solely to produce expert performers and perfect performance pieces. The process that students go through is of immense importance. It follows then that if the performance is to be a celebration of the school, its students and their achievements, then it should be about more than a pale re-creation of a popular musical or an attempt to 'cover' the latest hits.

If teachers keep sight of these facts and prepare for the performance in the same highly professional way that they prepare for other areas of the curriculum they will be rewarded with a hugely successful performance that will give immeasurable pleasure and benefit to all concerned and will leave students with memories that they carry with them for the rest of their lives.

This last chapter is dedicated to those we are all concerned about – the buggers we want to get in tune. This is what they had to say.

About their teachers

- 'He's a talented musician and this shows in his teaching. He's easy to talk to and music is very enjoyable in his lessons. He takes a practical approach rather than a written one.' (Amanda, Year 10 performing arts student)
- 'He's a good teacher and I find his lessons really interesting. I really enjoy music lessons much more now and am thinking about doing it for GCSE.' (Carl, Year 9)
- 'A really nice woman, a bit wacky, but she makes music a heck of a lot of fun. She probably knows everything about music in the world … but can't teach. She talks at us and expects us to understand.' (Suzanne, Year 10 GCSE music student)
- 'He's not that good at teaching but he can play instruments.' (Abid, Year 10 GCSE music student)
- 'A superb teacher with dazzling ideas. A wonder woman!' (Michael, Year 8)
- 'She's OK but never gives anyone in choir a chance to do solos. She always picks the same people and doesn't give us a chance! Other than that she is quite moody but really funny!' (Sinead, Year 10 GCSE music student)
- 'Amazing teacher, composer, arranger, and conductor … a general legend.' (Saira, Year 10 GCSE music student)

About their environment

- 'I like it best when we go on the computers.' (Dale, Year 9)
- 'They just stick us in the corridor, which is OK but it's not really music.' (Wesley, Year 8)
- 'They have some really good rooms but you have to wait 'til sixth form to get in them.' (Tom, Year 8)

165

- 'They've just built this new drama room; it's great for singing.' (Kate, Year 10 performing arts student)
- 'They haven't got enough headphones so you can't hear what you're doing.' (Deepa, Year 8)
- 'They put too many in one room it's mad.' (Holly, Year 9)
- 'Half the stuff is broken or there's a string missing.' (Kelly, Year 8)
- 'We can record CDs now so you can hear what you've done. My mum thinks it's great.' (Philip, Year 8) [/BL]

About music

- 'We did the music for the school play – that was really good.' (Amanda, Year 10 performing arts student)
- 'They made us play recorders – it was crap.' (Martin, Year 8 talking about Year 7)
- 'I find the theory part of it really hard but the composing is all right. We use Sibelius which is this software on the computer.' (Sinead, Year 10 GCSE music student)
- 'We've got this band and Mrs **** says we can play for the disco, which should be really good.' (Matthew, Year 10 GCSE music student)
- 'I like doing stuff that is modern like from films or off the radio.' (Bradley, Year 9)
- 'I used to think Beethoven was rubbish, I was right.' (Carl, Year 9)
- 'When you start doing music it's good how it all joins up, even the old stuff.' (Kate, Year 10 GCSE music student)

About themselves

- 'I really like playing. If I'm fed up or just bored it's really good to play.' (Abid, Year 10 GCSE music student)
- 'When I get it right it's a buzz.' (Wesley, Year 8)
- 'When I think about it I never thought I would stand up and sing in front of everyone. I was dead frightened but excited at the same time.' (Samantha, Year 8)

- 'I know I'm more confident now. I think it's the music.' (Michael, Year 8)
- 'I used to hate school but now I play keyboards and DJ they treat me differently.' (Marcus, Year 10 performing arts student)
- 'I couldn't read music for ages and then it just clicked. It's weird but I know what it means now.' (Saira, Year 10 GCSE music student)
- 'I don't think you have to learn to read [music] but it probably helps.' (Holly, Year 9)
- 'All my mates do music.' (Carl, Year 9)
- 'When you go to choir it's good cos all the years are there and they talk to you round the school.' (Deepa, Year 8)
- 'My boyfriend does music as well.' (Amanda, Year 10 performing arts student)
- 'My mum says she remembers music from school. I think I will as well.' (Bradley, Year 9)
- 'I don't know if I'll do it after but it would be good.' Marcus, Year 10 performing arts student)
- 'Maybe I'll get a job singing.' (Samantha, Year 8)

Appendix A

Some jobs in the world of music and what they entail

Performing artist: The range involved in this is infinite, ranging from amateurs through part-time professionals to full-time musicians. Jobs can be as a soloist or working with others. They may be in local clubs, big venues, cruise ships or holiday resorts at home and abroad. The list is almost endless. The best way to get work in this field is to get some experience and then try to get an agent.

Session musician: Usually very competent musicians who depend upon their reputations and a network of contacts to get work. Often they never become stars but they sometimes mix with the stars and provide the vital service of extra musical support for recording and live performance.

DJ: Mixes and plays records for public events. The days of a person with a few records and amplifier are gone. Being a DJ today means you really must know music. The best often make their own music and use up to the minute technology involving computers to create samples, mixes and multimedia music shows.

Technical support: Increasingly musical events need knowledgeable and talented people to make them work. Technicians who tune instruments, set up and maintain equipment, supervise recording, mix the sound and so on have now replaced the old fashioned 'roadie' who drove the van and carried the gear. Behind every successful music event is a team of specialists dealing with promotion, management, security, public relations and a host of other jobs vital to the success of the event. All of them, whatever their role, share a love of and an extensive knowledge of music and the processes that bring about its creation and performance.

Orchestra member and conductor: To work in this field the starting point has to be that you really have to be an outstanding musician. Given that this is well within the bounds of possibility, what are the opportunities? The Association of British Orchestras lists 58 different professional orchestras, ensembles and sinfoniettas among its members. Many are fully funded and permanent though some use freelance musicians as the need arises. The BBC alone has five orchestras and there are others based in or associated with the major cities of the UK, so providing quite a lot of opportunity (and even more so when one considers the international nature of music).

With regard to being a conductor, although it is a smaller field there are still many opportunities throughout the world, and as well as orchestras conductors can work with smaller groups and choirs. The Connexions website jobs4u gives an excellent outline of the career path a conductor might take.

Working for a record company: The face of this industry is changing considerably due to the influence of the internet and downloaded music. Although huge record companies still exist a lot more independent labels are springing up, some of which only make recordings in an electronic format for sale and promotion through the 'web'. The exact nature of the jobs available and the money earned will depend very much on the size and the success of the label. That said there are certain tasks that all labels will need to carry out so a prospective employee can expect to be involved in some or all of the following tasks. Once again a real love of music will be indispensable but since some of the jobs lean more to administration the use of music creatively won't necessarily play a significant part.

The label manager: In a large company the manager has the role of coordinator, steering policy and making sure that jobs are done on time and the label is maintaining its direction. He/she will have a large staff to do particular roles and some of those are listed below. In a smaller company the label manager will be much more 'hands on' and will be directly involved, usually doing a bit of everything from making the tea up.

A&R manager: A&R stands for artists and repertoire. This job involves talent scouting, going to lots of gigs, finding and signing the bands and getting them into the studio. It demands a good knowledge of music and requires real creative skill. An A&R person, through their choice of bands, determines the artistic direction of a label and gives it its identity.

A&R administrator: As the name implies a rather more 'admin' based job dealing with the budget for signing, recording and promoting bands but still likely to get to the gigs.

Marketing manager: More at the 'business' end of things, this person develops marketing plans for the label and the musician and then oversees the implementation of those plans.

Promotions: This usually involves a team of people who liaise with TV, radio and the Press to get exposure for the bands, their recordings, public appearances and so on. Within this section, depending on the size of the company, there could be all sorts of people, including *copy-writers* who write the press releases, *press officers* who actually contact the media, *style consultants* who will create a band's image, *designers* who will create logos, publicity posters and so on and *pluggers* who get mentions or airplay for the music on TV, radio and increasingly on the internet. If a label, because of its size or its policy, doesn't employ people in these roles full time, it will often employ commissioners to find designers, film makers and so on to do the required jobs.

Record producer: A producer is a vital person in the creative chain. It is they who will determine the final sound/feel of a piece of music by making decisions about what musicians/ instruments should be used, where microphones are placed and what the final mix and balance of the various tracks will be. All in all it is an extremely creative process. Producers are needed for every type of music. They work in recording studios, in live situations, in film and in television. While it is not absolutely essential to read music or to be a good performer it is important to have a good understanding of the musical process and without a pretty solid musical background it is unlikely that an aspiring producer will have the ear to hear the sound when they are mixing. Nowadays there are university courses available that will teach you what you need to know. Additionally you will need to understand computers and the software packages that are used for mixing and sampling tracks. The computer equipment and software are quite specialized so you will need to do a lot of research using specialist magazines like *Sound on Sound*. It is possible to start by using a PC but it must be one with a good processor and a lot of memory. Many people in the industry use Macintosh equipment so look carefully before buying. Once you know what you are doing it is possible to work from home. You won't sign up big bands by doing that but there is a lot of work available making demo tracks for up and coming artists and backing tracks for people who perform in clubs and medium sized venues.

Jobs associated with production and required in a recording studio include the *recording engineer* who sets up and maintains the equipment and a *programmer* who deals with all the software and computer equipment. In film, television and live theatre there is also the job of *sound designer* who is the person responsible for creating and recording sound tracks and sound effects.

Arranging: The interpretation of a piece of music through the arrangement is often what gives it a unique quality. To do this you need to have a good knowledge of music and have the ability to use sounds and instruments to build an arrangement. You will also need to be able to judge the performer and understand the genre in which they work so that your arrangement is appropriate to their needs and the audience's expectations. As with production there is plenty of scope in this area to work freelance or from home.

Composing: There is no substitute for hard work in this area and the sooner you start to compose the better. As well as being a good musician yourself you will need to make the effort to understand a range of musical styles and genres in order to give range variety and quality to your work. Many schools now use Cubase, which is a vital computer software tool for the composer. Additionally an understanding of Sibelius would help and a working knowledge of resources such as Sampletank. Not everyone will like your work and you will have to learn to be objective and to take criticism or rejection. There is never usually a fast track to success so be persistent and be patient. In terms of training there are increasing opportunities in school starting at the primary level. Many local authorities now run courses and summer schools in this type of work and there are good courses at a number of universities. Like so many other areas of music there is the chance to combine composing with other areas of work so it would be possible to do other things such as singer/ songwriter, lyricist, producer or arranger. If writing songs is not particularly your thing, then composing original works for film or theatre, writing advertising jingles or incidental music for promotional films or television might be other areas to look at.

Work in the media

People who have a passion for music but don't see themselves as performers often look to the media for a job. As with recording studios, radio and TV stations need producers so that is one route to take but there are other jobs besides. Many of the available jobs overlap and it is not uncommon to find radio presenters who are also music journalists and write books and articles on a regular basis. Equally people who start out by writing about music find their way into presenting for TV and radio or go on to work for internet sites.

Jobs in education

Teacher (schools): To do this you will need to do a degree in music with Qualified Teacher Status (QTS) or you will need to take a degree in music and follow it with a Post Graduate Certificate in Education (PGCE). To take the degree you will need to fulfil the basic university entry requirements and demonstrate your musical competence. This will usually involve an audition and a require-ment to pass music examinations to a particular level. The examinations in question will be the school examinations discussed in Chapter 3 and often evidence of competence in graded examinations with a board such as ABRSM. Work in this field will involve teaching music in line with the requirements of the National Curriculum. These will vary according to the area of the UK in which you teach. Some musicians spend their whole careers in school but it is also possible to move on and work for the local authority as an advisor/inspector or for Ofsted (the British government office for standards in education). Like all other areas of music you must have competence, you must love your subject and you must have the organizational and interpersonal skills that are essential to good teaching.

Other areas of teaching

As well as opportunities to teach in school there is the chance to work in colleges or in universities. To do this you will normally be required to have the at least the same level of qualification that is required in a school although universities may require further qualifications such as a degree at Masters level.

Peripatetic teaching: Many schools employ additional or peripatetic teachers to supplement their music provision. Often they will not require these teachers to have QTS but they will expect them to have graded qualifications, which give evidence of their competence. Many peripatetic teachers work in more than one school and also work as instrumental music teachers teaching private pupils outside school hours. Others are able to blend their teaching commitments with a career as a part-time professional performer.

Vocal coach: Teachers of singing are no different to any other instrumental music teacher and operate similar work patterns. In addition they often find themselves in demand to work as vocal coaches, either with aspiring singers or with existing professionals who want to get the most out of their voices.

Music therapist: As we said in the Introduction, music has a very special place within our culture in that it can reach so many people, including those with special needs. This quality means that music has a very particular role in enriching and/or changing the lives of children and adults with special needs including autism, speech disabilities, visual and aural difficulties, physical and mental disabilities or emotional and behavioural difficulty. There are times when these disabilities can be so severe that music is one of the few things that will make a difference. Therapists work in hospitals, hospices, prisons, schools and in the community. Currently there are seven postgraduate training courses in the UK that are approved by the British Society for Music Therapy. Admission to them usually requires qualification at degree level or equivalent in music, a high level of musical competence and suitable interpersonal skills. At present there are only about 300 registered therapists in the UK but this is an expanding area with international opportunities.

Associated jobs in the music business

Even if you are not necessarily a musician, if you have a real interest in music and want to be involved there are numerous jobs that would allow you to participate in the industry and make a vital contribution. Among them might be:

- **Accountant**: Assists those working freelance with their tax bills ensuring that they declare the correct level of earnings and gain appropriate tax exemption for materials, equipment and expenses incurred while working in their chosen area.
- **Agent**: Represents artists, getting them work and negotiating fees for that work.
- **Music lawyer**: Negotiates artists' contracts in recording, publishing, performing and associated areas. A lot of time is spent in meetings, negotiating and drafting contracts.
- **Manager (venue)**: Not essential to be a musician but might well work with musicians planning performances and dealing with a wide range of management and administrative tasks at the venue.
- **Manager (artist)**: Looks after the personal interests of an artist, helps them to plan their career, takes care of their work schedule and deals with all the logistical issues such as

175

transport, accommodation, appointments for appearances and so on. To do this job it would be preferable to have a good working knowledge of the music industry.
- **Music publisher**: Music publishing is a specialized area offering a variety of jobs related to promoting, marketing and copyrighting an artist's work.
- **Sales, promotion and marketing**: This is a vast area and encompasses all sorts of areas including advertising and promotional film making at one end and retail sales of music and instruments at the other.

Checklist for those with musical ambitions

- play as often as you can
- talk to professional musicians if you can
- research training options – find the one to suit you
- read about music
- listen to music
- have an action plan
- be honest with yourself
- know your strengths and develop them
- recognize your weaknesses and accommodate them
- things might go wrong – learn from it and move on
- have dreams, not fantasies
- have passion – work hard
- remember, being a pop star is not the only choice available!

Advice for advisors

One of the most important things when offering advice to aspiring musicians is not to let our concepts of life and happiness impinge upon the choices of those we are advising. It may be that the uncertainty of the creative world isn't for us; perhaps we aren't impressed with the salary structure, but all of that is irrelevant. We must make sure that we support ambition and not let our fears get in the way of someone else's future.

Appendix B

Useful websites

The Qualifications and Curriculum Authority (QCA, England) www.qca.org.uk

The Scottish Qualifications Authority (SQA), www.sqa.org.uk

The Council for the Curriculum, Examinations and Assessment (CCEA, Northern Ireland), www.ccea.org.uk

The Department for Education, Lifelong Learning and Skills (DELLS, Wales), http://new.wales.gov.uk (follow the links)

Incorporated Society of Musicians, www.ism.org/pdf/careers/pdf

Music for Schools Foundation, www.mfsf.org.uk

Careers advice

http://www.connexions-direct.com/
http://www.courses-careers.com/
http://www.electricbluesclub.co.uk/music_careers.html
http://www.ucas.com/

Music lessons

http://www.musiclessonsonline.co.uk/
http://www.abrsm.org
http://www.musicleader.net/

Index